W9-CBM-929

We Thank You, God, for These

We Thank You, God, for These

Blessings and Prayers for Family Pets

Anthony F. Chiffolo and
(The Rev.) Rayner W. Hesse, Jr.
Illustrated by Andrew Lattimore

Paulist Press
New York/Mahwah, N.J.

The authors have made every effort to use inclusive language wherever possible; however, when copyrights have required verbatim reproduction, the original language has been retained.

Cover design by Sharyn Banks
Book design by Lynn Else
Illustrations by Andrew Lattimore. Used with permission.

Copyright © 2003 by Anthony F. Chiffolo and Rayner W. Hesse, Jr.

All rights reserved. No part of this book may be reproduced or transmitted in any form or by any means, electronic or mechanical, including photocopying, recording, or by any information storage and retrieval system without permission in writing from the Publisher.

Library of Congress Cataloging-in-Publication Data

Chiffolo, Anthony F., 1959-
 We thank you, God, for these: blessings and prayers for family pets / Anthony F. Chiffolo and Rayner W. Hesse, Jr.
  p. cm.
 Includes bibliographical references.
 ISBN 0-8091-4125-6 (alk. paper)
 1. Prayers for animals. 2. Pet owners—Prayer-books and devotions—English. I. Hesse, Rayner W. II. Title.
 BV283.A63 C48 2003
 242′.88—dc21

                                                        2003010270

Published by Paulist Press
997 Macarthur Boulevard
Mahwah, New Jersey 07430

www.paulistpress.com

Printed and bound in the
United States of America

To all our pets, present and past,
who have taught us lessons of love
and life's wisdoms.

Apprehend God in all things, for God is in all things.
Every single creature is full of God
and is a book about God.
Every creature is a word of God.

—Meister Eckhart (c. 1260–c. 1327)

Contents

1

We Thank You, God, for These

In the fall of 2001, we were at the beach on Fire Island, New York. We had brought with us the ashes of Maggie, our seventeen-year-old chocolate Labrador retriever who had been put to sleep in January, to sprinkle them at the water's edge where she had spent lots of happy moments chasing sticks or other flotsam and jetsam every summer. With us were Nona, our fourteen-year-old chocolate Lab; Katie, our twelve-year-old chocolate Lab; and Lanie, our ten-month-old black Lab puppy, who had joyfully arrived at our home soon after Maggie's death. It was five o'clock on a fall afternoon, and we were the only creatures at the beach, save a few sea-gulls and deer peering over the dunes. When all our "family" was gathered, we took the lid off the small tin that held Maggie's ashes, and with dogs barking and birds flying over-head, each taking a turn, we let the trail of ash and bone ride its way from our hands and hearts to the littoral, and then on wind and wave out to sea. It was a simple ceremony, but just

1

and proper and full of reverence for a beautiful and loving animal who had been our long-time companion.

Because she had been sick for many months, the idea of holding a memorial service for Maggie had been on our minds. But the desire to honor her with a tribute in thanksgiving for the love she had shown us solidified in those final minutes at the vet's office when we received the news that heroic measures to prolong her existence would not translate into any quality of life. As she slipped away into a forever sleep while those who loved her gathered round, the letting go was overwhelming. The long-buried pain of past separations came rushing to the fore, and three adults plus a vet and his assistant were moved to tears.

Our reaction was somewhat startling and surprising at first. We had all grieved the loss of human companions and family members. Was this moment any different? Was its closeness to experiences we already knew what made it so poignant and so sacred? Was it right to feel so much sorrow? These questions required a lot of introspective thought; yet this most recent experience with death helped crystallize some deep feelings about how to express grief and loss, while finding a way to move beyond them.

The beginnings of a book about pet loss were already on the drawing table. Seventeen years of living next door to and then nearby the Hartsdale Canine Cemetery in Westchester County, New York, have brought many a call to officiate at funerals for a variety of animals, everything from dogs to cats to birds. With each petition comes special requests: "Can you do a Jewish prayer or blessing at the end?" "We're not overly religious, but we feel we ought to have some sort of special service. Is there any good poetry about animals you could read?" "Can you say a few kind words about our ferret?" And when all is done and the final words have been pronounced, those mourning the loss of their pet often ask for a copy of the service. So slowly through the years, a collection of thoughts and prayers has gathered itself into folders, waiting to be more formally organized.

When we first proposed the idea of a book about pet loss to a great cadre of publishers, the rejection was disheartening. One response began, "Once we stopped laughing, we were able to send you this letter." Other publishers thought there was no market for books on grieving the loss of pets. Still others said that our topic did not fit any of their publishing categories. Happily, Father Lawrence Boadt at Paulist Press saw the potential in our proposal, and thanks to his insights and knowledgeable direction, we have created *We Thank You, God, for These* as a response to the mandate given to humankind at creation, when we were charged with "dominion over the fish of the sea, and over the birds of the air, and over the cattle, and over all the wild animals of the earth, and over every creeping thing that creeps upon the earth" (Gen 1:26b). This book addresses some of the ways in which we are to carry out God's command.

Certainly, we can care for the creatures of the earth without bringing them into our homes. But the thousands of years that the human species has domesticated animals, making them our household and barnyard pets, place upon us the added responsibility of their nurture for as long as they live with us. We have taken them out of the environment where nature provides, so they have a life-long dependency on us. Therefore, the way in which we treat them and provide for them becomes the measure not only of our understanding of scripture, but also of just how civilized we are.

From a theological perspective, God's gift of dominion is set up in the image of God's realm, where all creatures have a place and all are good and deserving of love. Surely the creatures of God we call our pets are to be treated in our dominion with the love and compassion God has modeled for us.

As a response to this theological imperative and in acknowledgment of these biblical duties, we have written *We Thank You, God, for These* for pet lovers to use as a scriptural guide, a liturgical resource, and a reflection on the joys of living with animals as pets. This book also provides words of comfort at the time of the illness of our pets and words of solace and condolence for when our pets die.

The challenge, of course, is to understand the thoughts and feelings that arise when our pets depart from us. Do animals have souls? Do animals go to heaven? Probably no response from religious institutions would be adequate for those grieving the loss of their pet. Scripture, however, is more approachable. In the Bible we learn of God's love for all creation, and we learn the special part that animals play in bringing about God's realm, both in metaphor (as in "the lamb of God") and in daily life (as in "shepherds were watching their flocks by night"). God speaks through animals (Balaam's ass), sets people to their calling through animals

(Jonah and the whale), gives signs of the redemption of the world and offers hope through animals (the dove from Noah's ark), heals the sick through animals (the serpent lifted up in the wilderness), and in the tradition of the Church, surrounds the Savior of the world with animals at his birth (the oxen and the donkey in the stable). If animals themselves do not have souls, perhaps that is because they are very often the mind and the hand and the soul of *God*; and if heaven is where God is, then they are in a place where God will certainly continue to care for them.

There can be little doubt that we are animal lovers (we have four parakeets and two parrotlets, also). But writing this book has given us a new and even deeper appreciation of animals, especially those whom we call "our pets." They daily teach us the lessons that our world so desperately needs to learn about unconditional love, exuberance, affection, closeness, loyalty, and the comfort of "just being there." Without our pets, our life would be poorer; through them, we are convinced, we are more joyful, and if more joyful, much closer to God.

We thank you, God, for these blessings!

Anthony F. Chiffolo and
(The Rev.) Rayner W. Hesse, Jr.

2

What Does Scripture Say?

Eighty species of mammals, twenty-five kinds of birds, eight reptiles, and a dozen insects are found in scripture. To say that our biblical ancestors had a profound respect for nature, especially animals, is evidenced by these many scriptural passages that speak about sacrificial offerings, the humane treatment of all sorts of creatures, the importance of the continuation of the species, and the interaction between human workers and their animal counterparts. To the people of biblical times, animals were an essential and integral part of existence.

Often, the human characters in a biblical story were a reflection of the larger animal world of which they were but a small part. In the story of Jacob and his courting of the two daughters of Laban, we understand more fully which one held the greater interest by deciphering their Hebrew names: Leah ("antelope") and Rachel ("ewe"). Leah had an antelope's lovely eyes, but Rachel was shapely and beautiful like a young lamb, and Jacob was smitten with her. We know that the people under her charge were sure to pay attention to the judgments rendered by Deborah ("bee") because she sat under the tree with the hive just above her head. The names of Caleb ("dog"), Jonah ("dove"), and Latish ("lion") were indicative of their character and the roles they would play in their stories. The presence and spirit of animals were woven into the very fabric of everyday happenings, of daily life—of its very essence.

If asked about animals in the Bible, most everyone would recall the story of Noah's ark, the two-of-every-kind version from Genesis 6, God's insurance plan that all creating would not have to begin again at the point of primal dust. And in God's promises to Noah (Gen 9:3–16), it is proclaimed at least seven times that with every living soul and with all birds and cattle and beasts of the earth will the covenant be established. One need not be a theologian to understand that from the very beginning of creation and at the time of the covenant and from that moment forward, God has intended that we share the same space and in the same destiny as the other creatures that inhabit the earth.

But how are we to share, and what are the consequences of our actions or inactions? Why is our treatment of animals important to God? What special place do they have in the heart of God? To understand the theological nature of the relationship among God, humans, and our animal companions, a more in-depth look at some other biblical passages will be helpful.

What Does Scripture Say?
—A Look at Genesis

And God said, "Let the waters bring forth swarms of living creatures, and let birds fly above the earth across the dome of the sky." So God created the great sea monsters and every living creature that moves, of every kind, with which the waters swarm, and every winged bird of every kind. And God saw that it was good. God blessed them, saying, "Be fruitful and multiply and fill the waters in the seas, and let birds multiply on the earth."   *Gen 1:20–22*

So out of the ground the LORD God formed every animal of the field and every bird of the air, and brought them to the man to see what he would call them; and whatever the man called every living creature, that was its name. The man gave names to all cattle, and to the birds of the air, and to every animal of the field....   *Gen 2:19–20*

Then the LORD said to Noah, "Go into the ark, you and all your household.... Take with you seven pairs of all clean animals, the male and its mate; and a pair of the animals that are not clean, the male and its mate; and seven pairs of the birds of the air also, male and female, to keep their kind alive on the face of all the earth...." And Noah did all that the LORD had commanded him....

Of clean animals, and of animals that are not clean, and of birds, and of everything that creeps on the ground, two and two, male and female, went into the ark with Noah, as God had commanded Noah.

Gen 7:1–9

_____

Then [Noah] sent out the dove from him, to see if the waters had subsided from the face of the ground; but the dove found no place to set its foot, and it returned to him[,] to the ark, for the waters were still on the face of the whole earth. So he put out his hand and took it and brought it into the ark with him. He waited another seven days, and again he sent out the dove from the ark; and the dove came back to him in the evening, and there in its beak was a freshly plucked olive leaf; so Noah knew that the waters had subsided from the earth. Then he waited another seven days, and sent out the dove; and it did not return to him any more.

Gen 8:8–12

From the beginning of time, God had animals in mind. After the heavens and earth, the planets, and all types of vegetation were created, God set about the task of creating the waters and all the creatures who live therein, and all insects, reptiles, wild beasts, and birds. Seeing that this was good, and giving them the promise of a perpetual existence by means of God's blessing, God gave them their place as part of the eternal order of life. And in this order of things, the

animals of the world were created and received their blessing before God created a single human being, an order that
carries great theological importance. For though God did
give dominion over the earth and its creatures to us humans,
we need to take note of the created order and realize that it
is sacred.

Animals are high on God's list, and so they should be
for us. Time and again God demonstrates just how important
are the lions, ostriches, bears, leopards, whales, dogs, and
mice. When God destroyed the earth and all but eight of the
human species, at least two of every other species of animal
were saved by entering the ark. Noah and his family were to
care for them, just as God would, gathering them in as God
would and does. And before Noah's shipwrecked family
stepped even one foot onto the land where they would
rebuild their homes, God provided the dove with its nest,
making it the first inhabitant of a new earth.

What Does Scripture Say?
—A Look at Exodus

But the seventh day is a sabbath to the LORD your
God; you shall not do any work—you, your son or
your daughter, your male or female slave, your
livestock, or the alien resident in your towns.

Exod 20:10

When you come upon your enemy's ox or donkey
going astray, you shall bring it back. When you see

the donkey of one who hates you lying under its burden and you would hold back from setting it free, you must help to set it free.   *Exod 23:4–5*

Six days you shall do your work, but on the seventh day you shall rest, so that your ox and your donkey may have relief, and your homeborn slave and the resident alien may be refreshed.   *Exod 23:12*

Order is of great importance in the telling of the story of creation, and in the giving of God's laws it takes center stage. Before Moses went up the mountain, the Israelites had been taught that whatever God spoke was to be taken very seriously. Then when Moses came down the mountain with the tablets of the Law in his hands, the Israelites learned that what God had caused to be written was to be obeyed, or there would be grave consequences. Having left Egypt, where they were under the law of Pharaoh, the Israelites placed themselves under the new Law of the God who saved them, called them, and led them to the Promised Land.

In their rush to leave, they did not have time to let the bread rise, or to say goodbye; they had to leave many possessions behind. But, we note, the Israelites took their animals with them, and they established laws, backed by the power and authority of God's commandments, to keep these animals safe and healthy.

In the story of the Good Samaritan in the Gospel of Luke, Jesus challenged the hypocrisy of the Pharisees who knew that the Law demanded they pull a neighbor's donkey from the ditch. He knew that even on the Sabbath they would come to the aid of any of their own beasts of burden; yet they would decline to help an injured human "animal" lest they break God's Law. What we learn from the texts of Exodus and Luke are three things: (1) animals of burden, be they donkeys or horses or cattle, must not be overworked and must be treated with the same dignity we afford human beings; (2) animals deserve our respect and love, regardless of who owns them; and (3) the way God cares for animals is a prototype of how God loves us and how we should love one another.

We have a lot to learn from the animals that are our pets. When treated well—and, often, when not—their love is unconditional. We know from scripture that God's love is like this. And how we treat our pets is often a measure of our understanding and acceptance of God's love. Not only are our pets high on God's list, but their lives and their love are one of the many ways that God works through creation to speak to us.

What Does Scripture Say?
—A Look at Numbers

...[N]ow he [Balaam] was riding on the donkey, and his two servants were with him. The donkey saw the angel of the LORD standing in the road, with a drawn sword in his hand; so the donkey turned off the road, and went into the field; and

Balaam struck the donkey, to turn it back onto the road. Then the angel of the LORD stood in a narrow path between the vineyards, with a wall on either side. When the donkey saw the angel of the LORD, it scraped against the wall, and scraped Balaam's foot against the wall; so he struck it again. Then the angel of the LORD went ahead, and stood in a narrow place, where there was no way to turn either to the right or to the left. When the donkey saw the angel of the LORD, it lay down under Balaam; and Balaam's anger was kindled, and he struck the donkey with his staff. Then the LORD opened the mouth of the donkey, and it said to Balaam, "What have I done to you, that you have struck me these three times?" Balaam said to the donkey, "Because you have made a fool of me! I wish I had a sword in my hand! I would kill you right now!" But the donkey said to Balaam, "Am I not your donkey, which you have ridden all your life to this day? Have I been in the habit of treating you this way?" And he said, "No."

Then the LORD opened the eyes of Balaam, and he saw the angel of the LORD standing in the road, with his drawn sword in his hand; and he bowed down, falling on his face. The angel of the LORD said to him, "Why have you struck your donkey these three times? I have come out as an adversary, because your way is perverse before me. The donkey saw me, and turned away from me these three times. If it had not turned away from me, surely just now I would have killed you and let it live." Then Balaam said to the angel of the LORD, "I have sinned, for I did not know that you were standing in the road to oppose me."

Num 22:22–34

We all know of, have heard of, or have experienced cases of cruelty to animals. Whether through harsh words, a hand raised in frustration, or, as in the story of Balaam, a stick used as a weapon, animals too often bear the brunt of human anger. The writer of Numbers who related the story of Balaam's donkey cringed at its inhumane treatment. In a style reminiscent of Aesop's fables we encounter a beast of burden who not only speaks but also has the supernatural ability to see angels. The mere presence of God's messenger at the beginning of the story is a foreshadowing that the text will be both important to the hearer and sacred to God. As predicted, the donkey taught its master about the nature of patience and true obedience, the cruelty of anger, and the bounds of unconditional love.

At the outset, the presence of the angel of God informs us that this will be a story about someone or something whose life was in need of being saved. We quickly notice that the master showed no amazement that his donkey could speak, even less that it could reason, and still less that it might have insights worth sharing. Despite being struck three times, the donkey did not fight back nor turn and bite nor cast off its owner. In the end, the donkey demonstrated the attributes we would hope his master capable of, and it set its master, by this example, on a new journey of loving kindness. In addition, it is clear that the donkey saved its master from an angel of death. All the television animal shows in which Lassie or Flicka or Flipper make heroic rescues do not now seem so far-fetched—they have a biblical precedent. And we learn from this story what many already know—that animals have special insights, knowledge, and instincts that can be crucial to our well-being.

That the redactors of Numbers used the story of a donkey to convey this message is not unusual. The donkey figures in many memorable biblical passages: the sacrifice of Isaac, the story of Jesse, the Nativity narratives, the flight to Egypt, the parable of the Good Samaritan, and Jesus' triumphal entry into Jerusalem, to name a few. In each of these stories, the donkey is seen as the purveyor of the word or the carrier of the sacred, the lifter of the burden, the rescuer, or a metaphor for what is good and just in the world God has created. We see the great importance these helping animals have in the mind of God (perhaps even knowing the mind of God); and we discover that God does not condone cruelty for cruelty's sake in regard to a donkey or any animal, especially those that cannot speak to defend themselves. We also learn of the importance of living in harmony with the animal world: in other words, in God's realm we must care for our animals at least as well as they care for us.

What Does Scripture Say?
—A Look at Deuteronomy

But the seventh day is a sabbath to the LORD your God; you shall not do any work—you, or your son or your daughter, or your male or female slave, or your ox or your donkey, or any of your livestock, or the resident alien in your towns, so that your male and female slave may rest as well as you.

Deut 5:14

———————

You shall not plow with an ox and a donkey yoked together. *Deut 22:10*

———————

You shall not muzzle an ox while it is treading out the grain. *Deut 25:4*

Though we may not be aware of it, scripture does give space to quite a few verses that deal with the humane treatment of animals. It is clear from Deuteronomy, the second major book of the Law, that even more than two thousand years ago there was a concern by the elders of the tribes and the priestly lawmakers that animals not be overworked, that their workload be equal to their physical stature and strength, and that they receive just "payment" for good work. The place in the list in which they are ordered in Deuteronomy 5:14 demonstrates that their needs were to be considered even above those of the resident alien in town.

These prohibitions appear in Deuteronomy because animals had important status in the life of a God-fearing community. That the injunctions were connected to the priestly function means that there was a theological tie-in. In other words, the way in which the Israelites showed respect for their animals was a measure of their civilization, their moral code, and their respect for God and creation.

Lest the point seem too great a stretch, let us remember the work of Dr. Henry Bergh in a famous court case of 1874. Dr. Bergh, a long-time advocate of the humane treatment of animals, used his influence and the existing laws regarding the treatment of horses and other work animals to press for child-labor laws in the United States. Speaking on behalf of a young girl named Mary Ellen, he convinced the courts that while there was a law against beating or overworking an animal, it was cruel and insensitive not to afford the same protection to children working long hours in factories. But before he could get the court's attention, Bergh, one of the early forces behind the ASPCA, had first to prove that a child was, at the very least, an animal. His theological insights into how these passages from Deuteronomy spoke to the situation at hand formed the basis for child welfare reform and our current labor laws.

What Does Scripture Say?
—A Look at Job

"Do you give the horse its might?
    Do you clothe its neck with mane?
Do you make it leap like the locust?
    Its majestic snorting is terrible.

It paws violently, exults mightily;
  it goes out to meet the weapons.
It laughs at fear, and is not dismayed;
  it does not turn back from the sword.
Upon it rattle the quiver,
  the flashing spear, and the javelin.
With fierceness and rage it swallows the ground;
  it cannot stand still at the sound of the trumpet.
When the trumpet sounds, it says 'Aha!'
  From the distance it smells the battle,
  the thunder of the captains, and the shouting."

Job 39:19–25

The book of Job, and Job's battle with faith, his anger with God, and his attempts to be at peace with the world seem a strange place for a tribute to horses. In his struggle for courage in the face of utter despair, Job had need of a paradigm. He had no help from his friends, who had deserted him; his family had died; and even the plant he sat under to get out of the sun withered and was of no use. Where was inspiration to be found? Job found inspiration in the attributes of the horse. Clearly, the author is using the horse as a metaphor for the mighty warrior, the soldier who goes the distance, the fighter who perseveres. Once again, scripture insists that there are lessons to be learned by imitating and emulating domesticated animals.

Sometimes animals who become our pets inspire us with answers when there seem to be none. Sometimes the presence of an animal friend even calms the anger of an aching heart. When all others leave and hope seems distant, animal companions can remind us of love that stays, of love that sustains, of the kind of love we learn through faith in God. The author of Job found answers in an equine metaphor, and it brought him peace.

What Does Scripture Say? *—A Look at the Psalms*

The LORD is my shepherd, I shall not want.
　　He makes me lie down in green pastures;
he leads me beside still waters;
　　he restores my soul.
He leads me in right paths,
　　for his name's sake.
Even though I walk through the darkest valley,
　　I fear no evil;
for you are with me;
　　your rod and your staff—
　　they comfort me.
You prepare a table before me
　　in the presence of my enemies;
you anoint my head with oil;
　　my cup overflows.
Surely goodness and mercy shall follow me
　　all the days of my life,
and I shall dwell in the house of the LORD
　　my whole life long.　　　　　*Ps 23*

Holy people of God, revere Adonai—
  for those who stand in awe of God lack nothing.
The young lion may grow weak and hungry,
  but those who seek Our God will lack no good
    thing.   *Ps 34:9–10 IP*

―――――――――

Alleluia!
Praise Our God from the heavens,
  praise God in the heights!
Praise God, all you angels,
  praise God, all you hosts!
Praise God, sun and moon,
  praise God, all you shining stars!
Praise God, you highest heavens,
  and you waters above the heavens!
Let them praise the Name of Our God,
  by whose command they were created.
God established them forever and ever
  and gave a decree which won't pass away.
Praise Our God from the earth,
  you sea creatures and ocean depths,
lightning and hail, snow and mist,
  and storm winds that fulfill God's word,
mountains and all hills,
  fruit trees and all cedars,
wild animals and all cattle,
  small animals and flying birds,
rulers of the earth, leaders of all nations,
  all the judges in the world,

young men and young women,
  old people and children—
let them all praise the Name of Our God
  whose Name alone is exalted,
whose majesty transcends heaven and earth,
  and who has raised up a Horn for God's people
to the praise of the faithful,
  the children of Israel, the people dear to God!
Alleluia!   *Ps 148 IP*

In Psalm 23 the psalmist continues the use of animal metaphor we encounter in Job: Humanity is likened to a sheepfold, tended to by a great shepherd who has compassion for the flock amidst all conditions, from need to abundance, danger to peace, sorrow to great joy. The psalmist knows that a sheep recognizes its master's voice, follows its master when called, rejoices at its master's arrival—a metaphor intended to teach us that when we answer the call of the Shepherd, we, too, can come to know the love of a nurturing God.

Normally, the lion is a symbol of virility. But in Psalm 34, the young lion represents impetuous youth, whose impatience prevents it from capturing its prey. With this metaphor, the psalmist implies that those who seek God will capture all that they need and will lack nothing.

Having tired of metaphor, the psalmist approaches the end of the list of songs and in Psalm 148 plainly tells how the whole earth exalts its Creator. The animals who were created before humankind—sea creatures, wild animals, cattle, small animals, and flying birds—praise God for the gift of life. And if they praise God, how much more must the children of God do likewise?

What Does Scripture Say?
—A Look at Proverbs and Ecclesiastes

The righteous know the needs of their animals,
but the mercy of the wicked is cruel.

Prov 12:10

———————————

For the fate of humans and the fate of animals is the same; as one dies, so dies the other. They all have the same breath, and humans have no advantage over the animals; for all is vanity. All go to one place; all are from the dust, and all turn to dust again. Who knows whether the human spirit goes upward and the spirit of animals goes downward to the earth? So I saw that there is nothing better than that all should enjoy their work, for that is their lot; who can bring them to see what will be after them? *Eccl 3:19–22*

We have often heard that it's easy to trust someone who loves animals, and folk wisdom enjoins, "Don't trust a person who doesn't like pets." The writers of Proverbs and Ecclesiastes would agree, pointing to the special knowledge that all pet owners keep close to their hearts: the needs of their animals and the unique spirit they bring to a home. In these Wisdom

Books' passages, the wise and righteous person is one who loves his or her pets. So, simply put, in the thoughts of the scripture writers, good human beings care for animals.

But why should we long to be good in this way? What do animal lovers intuit that others don't? The writer of Ecclesiastes provides us with a possible answer. In the end, all animals, human or otherwise, suffer the same fate, returning, without partiality, to the dust from which we have been created. Spirit is spirit, whether human or not, so we best attend in like manner to all spirit that emanates from and returns to the One God. Whether in flesh or in dust, God has made us kindred spirits through the act of creation, and surely, we should be respectful of that kinship.

Yet many people profess that only humans have a spirit and only human spirits can go to heaven. To pet lovers, the idea that animals remain earthbound seems cruel, and unlike the mercy of God. God gifted us with our animal companions, and as they enter into communion with our spirits, surely they will remain connected with us for all eternity. If this bond between humans and animals makes life good or better, then the relationship should be cultivated. All of creation is connected, one life to another. The more we learn this and respect it, the more whole we, and the earth on which we live, will be.

What Does Scripture Say?
—A Look at Matthew

"Therefore I tell you, do not worry about your life, what you will eat or what you will drink, or about your body, what you will wear. Is not life more than food, and the body more than clothing? Look at the birds of the air; they neither sow nor reap nor gather into barns, and yet your heavenly Father feeds them. Are you not of more value than they? And can any of you by worrying add a single hour to your span of life? And why do you worry about clothing? Consider the lilies of the field, how they grow; they neither toil nor spin, yet I tell you, even Solomon in all his glory was not clothed like one of these. But if God so clothes the grass of the field, which is alive today and tomorrow is thrown into the oven, will he not much more clothe you— you of little faith? Therefore do not worry, saying, 'What will we eat?' or 'What will we drink?' or 'What will we wear?'…But strive first for the kingdom of God and his righteousness, and all these things will be given to you as well.

"So do not worry about tomorrow, for tomorrow will bring worries of its own. Today's trouble is enough for today."   *Matt 6:25–34*

"Are not two sparrows sold for a penny? Yet not one of them will fall to the ground apart from your Father….you are of more value than many sparrows."   *Matt 10:29, 31b*

Undoubtedly among the most recognizable parts of the New Testament, these passages from Matthew spotlight the birds of the air (the swallows that gather into barns, and the sparrows). They are not required to plant their own food, nor cut it, nor store it, and they are not concerned with what is to come, how much is enough, or the price for storing food. God provides for them amply.

Matthew's knowledge of the Hebrew scriptures shows through in these passages. In Psalm 84:3, swallows and sparrows portray the peace and tranquility of the Jerusalem Temple: "The sparrow has found its home at last, / the swallow a nest for its young—..." (IP). Their humility and fragility are among the reasons they are so special to God. For Jews who were required to make sacrifices at the Temple, sparrows were the most insignificant and least costly offering; in fact, they were known as the leper's offering, the presentation before God from a poor beggar. The tiny swallow that builds a nest of mud in such humble places as under the eaves of barns was also seen as a symbol of lowliness, a representation of those whose search for sustenance never ceases. Yet God knows their needs and provides for them plenty. In Matthew, the sparrows and the swallows became a metaphor for God's all-encompassing love for us. For are we not part of creation, and at the very least equal in the stature of God's eye to the birds that fly above us?

The pattern of learning from animals established in the Hebrew scriptures continues in Matthew. The text's use of metaphor and everyday experience with animals impart to us lessons about humility, about peace of mind, about unnecessary worry—about placing ourselves in God's hands and trusting in God's providence. Without animals, life's lessons would be even more difficult to understand, life's trials even more difficult to bear.

What Does Scripture Say?
—A Look at Mark

A woman whose young daughter had an unclean spirit heard about him. She approached Jesus and fell at his feet. The woman, who was Greek, a Syro-Phoenician by birth, begged Jesus to expel the demon from her daughter.

He told her, "Let the children of the household satisfy themselves at table first. It is not right to take the food of the children and throw it to the dogs."

She replied, "Yes, Rabbi, but even the dogs under the table eat the family's scraps."

Then Jesus said to her, "For saying this, you may go home happy; the demon has left your daughter." When she got home, she found her daughter in bed and the demon gone.   *Mark 7:25–30 INT*

Then Jesus told them, "Go into the whole world and proclaim the Good News to all creation."

Mark 16:15 INT

Dogs are mentioned more than forty times in the Bible, not always in a favorable light. This is due most likely to the fact that the Egyptians worshiped dogs (and cats), and they were so highly regarded that Pharaoh and his people considered them a desirable repository for the human soul at the time of death. To the Israelites, anything Egyptian or outside of the Jewish cult of worship was suspect.

In Jesus' exchange with the Syro-Phoenician woman, we see that anything relating to the Gentiles was also suspect. They, like the dogs, were not deemed worthy to even gather up the crumbs under the Master's table. In his cleverly sarcastic rebuke, Jesus underlined his insult with timeworn arguments and clichés. The woman had been bold; she had dared to approach a man in public and speak to him—an unacceptable taboo and sacrilege.

Not to be undone, for the life of her daughter was at stake, she demonstrated that she was equal to Jesus' word play and challenged him with a surprisingly adept comeback. Humbling herself, she accepted the canine insult with a disarming self-deprecation in the manner of David before Saul (1 Sam 24:14). Amazed at her intelligence and tenacity, and impressed with her ability to rise above the prevailing prejudices to achieve her purpose, Jesus healed her daughter and sent her on her way.

In the end, Jesus' actions in this story contravened the norms and expectations of the ruling religious class where he talked and walked, but he first had to take a page from the very one whose presence conjured images of a begging dog. Jews of the biblical era believed that the dog was an animal to be avoided at all costs. In some Mid-Eastern societies today, it is still considered the greatest of insults to call another person a dog. In the paradox that is typical of Jesus' preaching and teaching, the canine insult that was meant to injure became the vehicle of healing. It is the presence of a dog in the story that allows the same healing solace to comfort Lazarus at the gate in Luke 16. After examining the stories in Mark and Luke, we can begin to understand how dogs came to be a prototype in the New Testament of the outcast who is ushered in, the prodigal son who is welcomed home, the woman at the well who is blessed by Jesus—signs of the all-inclusiveness of God's reign. We see the way in which a new message of universality swept through the early Church, turning it upside down, transforming it, and imbuing it with a fresh and life-giving attitude. Now the good news was to be proclaimed to *all* creation, including those formerly left out, kept out, driven out.

What Does Scripture Say?
—A Look at John

"And just as Moses lifted up the serpent in the wilderness, so must the Son of Man be lifted up, that whoever believes in him may have eternal life."   *John 3:14–15*

Peter said to him, "Lord, why can I not follow you now? I will lay down my life for you." Jesus answered, "Will you lay down your life for me? Very truly, I tell you, before the cock crows, you will have denied me three times."   *John 13:37–38*

Snakes and roosters are not the first animals that might come to mind when people think about pets. Yet we know that people have taken as pets animals that are generally found in the zoo, on the farm, and in the wild. Though cats and dogs, birds and fish are the most common "domesticated" animals, we all know someone who calls their ferret or their iguana or their goose their best mate, their fond companion. Even the more scary and malevolently perceived of reptiles are loved and cared for by doting owners.

And why not? Take the much-maligned snake, the serpent of biblical yore. In one form or another it is mentioned seventy times in scripture, and its poisonous venom some fifty times as well. Yet the early Church championed the snake as both a symbol of new life (due to its ability to shed its skin) and salvation, prefiguring the saving nature of Christ's crucifixion, as seen in the passage above, which hearkens back to the days of Moses. In Numbers 21:6–9, the Israelites were suffering from a plague of serpents literally biting at their heels. Crying out for help, Moses was instructed by God to fashion a snake of bronze and raise it up on a pole so that all who had been afflicted could gaze upon it. Those who looked upon it in faith were healed—a spectacular miracle of God's grace granted to the obediently faithful. Like other biblical writers, the author of the Gospel of John used the serpent story as an allegory to explain the expiatory and healing nature of Jesus' death on the cross. If the snake, thought to be evil, when lifted up, became the agent of healing, how much more so would the man, the son of God, subjected to the evil horrors of the cross, when lifted up, bring healing to the world he gazed down upon? Is it a wonder that the symbol for the medical profession, the caduceus, is a staff with two intertwining snakes?

And though roosters may conjure in the minds of many the terribly brutal cockfights of backroom gambling, they too have a prominent place in the symbolism of healing and resurrection theology. In Peter's story, the rooster's presence embodied a seemingly ominous turn of events. His cowardly denial of Jesus was more chicken than cocksure. But like the oft-disreputable serpent, the cock's crow was redeemed by God's plan. What was once a sinister foreboding of doom and death now signaled the coming of dawn and the return of life to the earth. As a symbol of watchfulness and patient waiting, it has found its place on church steeples and weather-vaned buildings and is the emblem for the emerging first-century Church under the direction of Peter, who heard its call.

We see that taken together, and as part of a nontraditional group of pets, snakes and roosters and everything under heaven have a purpose, and that the presence of each is important to the working out of God's plan.

> "For everything God created is good, and nothing is to be rejected provided thanksgiving is given for it; it is made holy by the word of God and prayer."
>
> *1 Tim 4:4 INT*

3

Blessings and Prayers for Animals

As a society, we have extended blessings to a wide variety of circumstances, events, and things. We bless the beginnings of journeys, we bless relationships, we even bless houses and cars and boats. Can we bless animals? Certainly, if we look at the essence of blessing—wishing the recipient vitality, health, longevity, and fertility, among other goods—it makes more sense to bless a cat or dog or gerbil than it does to bless a battleship.

The same holds true for prayer. If we can petition God for the well-being of our businesses, then we can certainly ask God to keep our pets safe from harm.

As we learned in the scriptures we have already examined, blessings are a fundamental expression of the inheritance we receive from God, and prayers are our dialogue with the Divine to help us understand the nature of our blessings. What follow are some simple blessings and prayers that sanctify our relationship with our animal companions.

For All Animals

We beseech you, O Lord,
to hear our supplication
on behalf of the whole creation,
who after their kind, bless, praise,
and magnify you forever.
Grant that all cruelty may
cease out of our land and deepen
our thankfulness to you for the
faithful companionship of
those whom we delight to call
our friends.   *Royal Society for the Prevention*
                      of Cruelty to Animals, adapted

O God, Creator of all things bright and beautiful,
we ask your blessings this day on all that is before
you, all that is before us, as we gaze upon a world
created so that we might live, and move, and have
our being. Bless all living things around us, especially the animals that you have given into our
care, that our interaction may be one of peace and
harmony in living; help us to learn from them, and
they from us, about your purpose for this world;
and may we remember that we are created from
that same primal dust, to which we all return. In a
life replete with challenges, a life of joy and sadness, of great gatherings and lonely places, surround us with the Spirit of mutual respect, one for

the other, and make us companions along the way.

Rayner W. Hesse, Jr.

Could I name them all,
My kindred spirits?

Wolves,
Husky dogs,
Deer,
Kingfishers—
    these thrill my soul.
Dolphins,
Swallows
    gladden my heart;
Seahorses,
Giraffes
    amuse, and
    awe.

Yet why these?
Is not the grizzly as noble,
The hummingbird as graceful,
The kangaroo as queer?

Do we all have our favorites?
You prefer cheetahs, swans, and starfish—
What do they have
    in common
    one with another,
    each with you?

Is the connection mere experience—
The swallows, when I was a boy, built nests
   beneath the eaves
   outside my bedroom window—
Or a matter of aesthetics?
But I know no giraffes in person...

Something speaks to us—
The wolf's wildness to me, perhaps
The starfish's symmetry to you—
Maybe a longing
For something missing
From our narrow lives,
Something important,
And terrific,
Which we cannot name,
Yet still recognize
   within,
   at the surging of our blood
When we,
   by chance,
Spy a butterfly
Flutter past.

Anthony F. Chiffolo

Creator God, Source of All, we know that you
delight in creatures as diverse as angelfish and
zebras, for we, made in your image, do too.
Remind us that as images of you, we also are cre-
ators, responsible for shaping a world where oys-

ters and ocelots and all animals can flourish.
Guide and bless our creative efforts, we pray, that
we may cherish and serve cranes and crawfish,
chipmunks and caribou, and all the spectacular
diversity of life that abides in the waters, on the
land, and in the air. Amen.   *Anthony F. Chiffolo*

Eternal God, Creator of all human life, parent of
the universe, help us fulfill our obligation to
replenish the world. Teach us the sanctity of all
life that we may truly serve as partners with you in
the daily act of creation. May we learn to manifest
our love for you through loving all of your creation. May we become messengers of your loving
concern now and forever.   *Rabbi Harold S. White*

Deep peace of the running wave to you.
Deep peace of the flowing air to you.
Deep peace of the quiet earth to you.
Deep peace of the shining stars to you.
Deep peace of the infinite peace to you.
                Celtic blessing attributed to Fiona McLeod
                [William Sharp, 1855–1905]

O God, I thank thee
for all the creatures thou hast made,
so perfect in their kind—
great animals like the elephant and the rhinoceros,
humorous animals like the camel and the monkey,
friendly ones like the dog and the cat,

working ones like the horse and the ox,
timid ones like the squirrel and the rabbit,
majestic ones like the lion and the tiger,
for birds with their songs.
O God, give us such love for thy creation,
that love may cast out fear,
and all thy creatures—and thy creation—
see in men and women like us
their priest and their friend....

George Appleton [1902–93]

Dearest Saint Francis, inspire us to see God's fingerprints in all of creation, especially in the animals with which we share our world. Teach us how to talk with birds as you did, to coexist with wolves, to treat fish with kindness, to comfort rabbits—to be people of peace in relation to all of God's creatures. Instill in us your extravagant love of every living thing. Amen. *Anthony F. Chiffolo*

For Our Pets

Prayer for My Pet
In your infinite wisdom, Lord God, when you created the universe, you blessed us with all living creatures. We especially thank you for giving us our pets who are our friends and who bring us so much joy in life. Their presence very often helps us get through trying times. Kindly bless my pet.

May my pet continue giving me joy and remind me of your power.

May we realize that as our pets trust us to take care of them, so we should trust you to take care of us, and in taking care of them we share in your love for all your creatures. Enlighten our minds to preserve all endangered species so that we may continue to appreciate all of your creation.

Grant this through Christ our Lord. Amen.

author unknown

———————————

Lord, you love the animals as you love your children. We give thanks for how you use them to teach us lessons of your unconditional love and forgiveness. Help us to be kind to the creatures you put in our care, as they look to us in the same manner that we look to you.

Lord, teach us patience and understanding so that we will seek to find all that is good about these creatures.

We thank you for the life of every pet and ask you to prepare a warm and happy place for them where they may know of your love and find rest within the shadows of your care. Amen. *author unknown*

———————————

God, around this table we are gathered as friends and family to give thanks for many things. Let us in our thoughts today especially remember the pets who are our companions. May they never be hungry while in our care, and may they always know and feel and come to understand that our table is set with them in mind also. For we believe, O God, that you have prepared a place for us, and in imitation of your love, we should prepare a place for those we love. May all at this table—under, around, and near it—be blessed with joy in your creation. How great are your works, O God! How wonderful are your deeds! Amen.   *Rayner W. Hesse, Jr.*

We call upon you, most blessed Saint Anthony, patron of domestic animals, to bless our pets this day. Protect them from injury, preserve them from illness, and help us provide all that they need. But more than that, inspire us to love them as they love us—unconditionally, unwaveringly, and always. Amen.   *Anthony F. Chiffolo*

For the Continued Health of Our Pets

Good Saint Francis, you loved all of God's creatures. To you they were your brothers and sisters. Help us to follow your example of treating every living thing with kindness. Saint Francis, patron saint of animals, watch over my pet and keep my companion safe and healthy. Amen.   *traditional*

O God, source of life and power, who feeds the birds of the heavens, increase our tenderness toward all in your care. Help us to refrain from petty acts of cruelty, or thoughtless deeds of harm to any living animal. May we care for them at all times, especially during hard weather, and protect them from injury so that they learn to trust us as friends. Let our sympathy grow with knowledge, so that the whole creation may rejoice in your presence.

author unknown

O Saint Hippolytus, we thank you for keeping our pets in your care. Please continue to bless them, we pray, that they might remain healthy and vigorous for all the years to come. Amen.   *Anthony F. Chiffolo*

For Newborn Animals

For a New Arrival

Little cries and whimpers, cooing, barks, and
    mews,
Mark the entry in our home, proclaim the
    newborn's news,
A bright-eyed pup, a small sweet bird, a warm
    and cuddly kitten
Has made its way here from some shop, and now
    we're totally smitten!
Yet give us courage to see beyond those big and
    longing eyes
To pause and thank you, God, for this: our
    beautiful pet surprise.

May we be blessed with life-long health, and it,
    too, in our care,
When you are near, God, and I am near, few
    burdens may it bear.   *Rayner W. Hesse, Jr.*

Mildest Saint Mildburga, like Saint Francis who communed with the birds, you had a special connection with our winged companions. So we ask you to watch over our feathered friends, especially all of this season's newly hatched chicks. Bless them with health of body and strength of spirit, that they may grow joyful in proclaiming God's love to all creation. Amen.   *Anthony F. Chiffolo*

O sweet Saint Gall, patron of the birds of the air, bless these newborn creatures that have been entrusted to our care. Ask the Lord to give them health and strength and length of days, and give us wisdom to provide for them in every way. Teach us to be patient with their youthful energy, and show us how to cherish them with love eternally. Amen.

Anthony F. Chiffolo

Holy Spirit, Breath of Life, bless all these newborns with health of body and strength of spirit, so that they may bring joy and love to all who are blessed with their companionship. Amen.

Anthony F. Chiffolo

For Sick Animals

Heavenly Father, our human ties with our friends of other species is a wonderful and special gift from You. We now ask You to grant our special animal companions your Fatherly care and healing power to take away any suffering they have. Give us, their human friends, new understanding of our responsibilities to these creatures of Yours. They have trust in us as we have in You; our souls and theirs are on this earth together to give one another friendship, affection, and caring. Take our petition for these, Your ill or suffering animals. Take our heartfelt prayers and fill them with healing light and strength to overcome whatever weakness of body they have.

(Here mention the names of the animals needing prayer.)

Your goodness is turned upon every living thing; Your grace flows to all Your creatures. From our souls to theirs goodness flows out and touches each of us with the reflection of Your love. To our special animal companions grant long and healthy lives. Give them good relationships with us, and if You see fit to take them from us, help us to understand that they are not gone from us, but only drawing closer to You. Grant our prayer through the intercession of good Saint Francis of Assisi, who honored You through all Your creatures. Give him the power to

watch over our animal friends until they are safely
with You in eternity, where we someday hope to join
them in giving You honor forever. Amen.

Gloria Pinsker

––––––––––

O God, we ask your blessing
On all that we hold dear:
The animal we're caressing
Who loves us without fear,
This pet whose heart's not guessing
'Bout who should hold it near.
It's you and me, God, pressing
Close a soul whose cries we hear.

Rayner W. Hesse, Jr.

––––––––––

O holy Saint Roch, in remembrance of the dog
who helped you recover from your own illness, we
implore your blessing upon our dear _____. Send
your spirit of healing to this sick animal, and ask
our Creator to cure _____ so that we may once
again delight together in the joy that God has
placed in our hearts. Amen. *Anthony F. Chiffolo*

––––––––––

We invoke your name, most blessed Saint Dwyn,
for the healing of this sick creature. Your intercession has already brought about the cures of
countless animals, so we ask for your prayers on
behalf of our beloved _____, who is precious to
us. Bless *her/him* and ask God to take away *her/his*
malady and restore *her/him* to full health. O dear

saint, please keep _____ under your watchful eye. Amen.   *Anthony F. Chiffolo*

_____

O God, my heart is sad because _____, my _____, is sick and nothing can be done to heal *her/him*. _____ has been with me for so long, and now *she/he* will be leaving me—and taking part of my heart with *her/him*. I ache already from the empty hole _____'s death will create in my life. But more than that, I cry because _____ is in pain. Please, God, don't let *her/him* suffer. Help me to show _____ that I love *her/him*, to comfort *her/him* when death comes, to be _____'s companion until the very end. And when the unfortunate inevitable comes to pass, to remember _____ with love and keep *her/his* memory with me forever. Amen.

Anthony F. Chiffolo

For Animals That Have Died

Do not stand at my grave and weep.
I am not there, I do not sleep.
I am a thousand winds that blow.
I am the diamond glint on snow.
I am the sunlight on ripened grain.
I am the gentle autumn rain.
When you awake in morning's hush,
I am the swift uplifting rush
of quiet birds in circled flight.

I am the soft stars that shine at night.
So do not stand by my grave and stare:
I am not there. I'm in God's care.

Mary E. Frye, adapted

———————

Lord God, to those who have never had a pet, this prayer will sound strange, but to you, Lord of all life and Creator of all creatures, it will be understandable.

My heart is heavy as I face the loss in death of my beloved _____, who was so much a part of my life.

_____ made my life more enjoyable and gave me cause to laugh and to find joy in *her/his* company. I remember _____'s fidelity and loyalty and will miss *her/his* being with me. From _____ I learned many lessons, such as quality of naturalness and the unembarrassed request for affection. In caring for _____'s daily needs, I was taken up and out of my own self-needs and thus learned service to others.

May the death of _____ remind me that death comes to all of us, animal and human, and that it is the natural passage for all life. May _____ sleep on in eternal slumber in your godly care as all creation awaits the fullness of liberation. Amen.

Edward Hays

———————

You fought hard to stay alive, my friend. In the end, though, you couldn't conquer death. But neither did death conquer you. Death cures all diseases, mends all broken bones, breaks all chains. And made you free at last. *author unknown*

—————

Farewell, master, yet not farewell
Where I go, ye too shall dwell
I am gone, before your face
A moment's time, a little space
When ye come where I have stepped
Ye will wonder why you wept.

Edwin Arnold [1832–1904]

—————

He Is Not Dead
I cannot say, and I will not say
That he is dead. He is just away.
With a cheery smile, and a wave of the hand,
He has wandered into an unknown land
And left us dreaming how very fair
It needs must be, since he lingers there.
And you—oh, you, who the wildest yearn
For an old-time step, and the glad return,
Think of him faring on, as dear
In the love of There as the love of Here.
Think of him still as the same, I say,
He is not dead—he is just away.

James Whitcomb Riley [1852–1916]

—————

May the God who created us and you, the God whose Spirit renews the face of the earth, the God who lent you to us, _____, as our companion for a time, now receive you back into heaven's tender care and keeping. Amen.

adapted from a prayer by John Miles Evans

4

Services for Blessing Animals

We gather together as communities of worship to bless the important events and relationships of our lives. As the Gospel of Mark entreats us to "go into all the world and proclaim the good news to the whole creation" (16:15), it is fitting that we should gather together to bless our animal companions and our relationships with our pets. Traditionally, communities of worship have held ceremonies for blessing animals on the feast of St. Francis of Assisi, the patron saint of animals, known as such because he is said to have talked with birds, fish, rabbits, and even a wolf. What follows are two communal services for blessing animals on the feast of St. Francis.

The Blessing of the Animals on the Feast of St. Francis of Assisi (October 4)

At the opening, all gather outdoors or in the church with their pets. When all are in place, the following is said in unison:

At the Opening: "Canticle of the Sun"

Most high, omnipotent, good Lord,
Praise, glory, honor, and benediction—all are
   yours.
To you alone do they belong, Most High,
And there is no one fit to mention you.

Praise be to you, my Lord, with all your creatures,
Especially to my worshipful brother sun,
Who lights up the day, and through him do you
   give brightness;
And beautiful is he and radiant with great
   splendor;
Most High, he represents you to us.

Praised be my Lord for sister moon and for the
   stars,
In heaven you have formed them clear and
   precious and fair.

Praised be my Lord for brother wind
And for the air and clouds and fair and every
   kind of weather,

By whom you give to your creatures nourishment.
Praised be my Lord for sister water,
Who is greatly helpful and humble and precious
    and pure.

Praised be my Lord for brother fire,
By whom you light up the dark.
And fair is he and gay and mighty and strong.

Praised be my Lord for our sister, mother earth,
Who sustains and keeps us
And brings forth diverse fruits with grass and
    flowers bright.
Praised be my Lord for those who for your love
    forgive
And bear weakness and tribulation.
Blessed those who shall in peace endure,
For by you, Most High, shall they be crowned.

Praised be my Lord for our sister the bodily
    death,
From whom no living person can flee.
Woe to them who die in mortal sin;
Blessed those who shall find themselves in your
    most holy will,
For the second death shall do them no ill.

Praise you and bless you, my Lord, and give him
    thanks,
And be subject to him with great humility.

St. Francis of Assisi [1182–1226]

The people may be seated for the lessons.

A Reading from Genesis 1:1, 20–25

In the beginning God created heaven and earth….[And] God said, "Let the waters be alive with a swarm of living creatures, and let birds wing their way above the earth across the vault of heaven." And so it was. God created great sea-monsters and all the creatures that glide and teem in the waters in their own species, and winged birds in their own species. God saw that it was good. God blessed them, saying, "Be fruitful, multiply, and fill the waters of the seas; and let the birds multiply on land." Evening came and morning came, the fifth day.

God said, "Let the earth produce every kind of living creature in its own species; cattle, creeping things and wild animals of all kinds." And so it was. God made wild animals in their own species, and cattle in theirs, and every creature that crawls along the earth in its own species. God saw that it was good. *NJB*

Psalm 84:1–3

How lovely is your dwelling place, O LORD of hosts!
My soul longs, indeed it faints for the courts of
   the LORD;

my heart and my flesh sing for joy to the living
   God.
Even the sparrow finds a home, and the swallow
   a nest for herself,
where she may lay her young,
at your altars, O LORD of hosts…

A Reading from the Book of Job (12:1, 7–9)

Then Job answered:…
"But ask the animals, and they will teach you;
the birds of the air, and they will tell you;
ask the plants of the earth, and they will teach you;
and the fish of the sea will declare to you.
Who among all these does not know
that the hand of the LORD has done this?"

All stand and join together in the following hymn.

"All Things Bright and Beautiful" (sung or said)

(Refrain) All things bright and beautiful, all
   creatures great and small;
All things wise and wonderful, the Lord God
   made them all.

Each little flower that opens, each little bird that
   sings,

he made their glowing colors, he made their tiny
wings. *(Refrain)*

The purple-headed mountain, the river running by,
the sunset, and the morning that brightens up
the sky. *(Refrain)*

The cold wind in the winter, the pleasant
summer sun,
the ripe fruits in the garden, he made them every
one. *(Refrain)*

He gave us eyes to see them, and lips that we
might tell
how great is God Almighty, who has made all
things well. *(Refrain)*

Words: Cecil Frances Alexander [1818–95];

Tune: "Royal Oak"

A Reading from the Gospel According to Luke (15:3–6)

[Jesus] told them this parable: "Which one of you, having a hundred sheep and losing one of them, does not leave the ninety-nine in the wilderness and go after the one that is lost until he finds it? When he has found it, he lays it on his shoulders and rejoices. And when he comes home, he calls together his friends and neighbors, saying to them, 'Rejoice with me, for I have found my sheep that was lost.'"

A short homily may be preached on the theme for the day. In place of a homily, especially if many children are present, reflections on the following story of St. Francis and the wolf may be appropriate:

> Saint Francis addressed [the Wolf] in these words, saying: "...I desire, Brother Wolf, to make peace between you and [the people], so that you may offend no more, and they shall forgive you all your past offences....I promise you that I will see to it that your living shall be given you continually, so long as you shall live, by the men of this country, so that you shall not suffer hunger; forasmuch as I am well aware that hunger has caused your every crime. But since I get for you this grace, I require, Brother Wolf, your promise never again to do harm to any human being, neither to any beast. Do you promise?"...the Wolf lifted up his right paw and confidingly laid it in the hand of Saint Francis, giving him this pledge of his faith....
>
> *The Little Flowers of Saint Francis*

At the conclusion of the homily, the following prayer is recited in unison by the entire congregation, kneeling:

A Prayer for Animals

Hear our humble prayer, O God, for our friends the animals, especially for animals who are suffering, for any that are hunted or lost or deserted or frightened or hungry; for all that must be put to death. We entreat all Thy mercy and pity, and for those who deal with them we ask a heart of compassion and gentle hands and kindly words. Make us, ourselves, to be true friends to animals and so to share the blessings of the merciful.

Albert Schweitzer [1875–1965]

Other suitable prayers may then be recited by the celebrant. The sign of peace is then exchanged (all stand):

Celebrant: The peace of God be always with you.
People: And also with you.

If there is to be a communion, it occurs at this point. At the conclusion of the communion (or if there is no communion), the service continues with the blessing of the animals. The animals, now gathered in one place, receive a communal blessing from the celebrant using one of the following general blessings:

O Supreme Spirit of Creation,
    from Your sacred breath came forth
    birds and beasts, fish and fowl,
    creatures of such variety and beauty
    that we are continuously amazed
    at Your divine imagination.
These children of Yours
    have been blessed by You, their Creator,
    with simplicity, beauty and a cosmic purpose.

They have been blessed as well
    by our greatest grandfather, Adam,
    who in Edenland gifted each with its own name.
They have also been blessed with protection
    by our ancient ancestor Noah,
    patron saint of those
    who seek to preserve all that You have created.
Sheep and goats, donkeys and cows,
    doves and serpents, fish and birds of the air
    were blessed by Jesus, Your Son,
    by His being born in their company
    and by His making use of them in
    His teachings.   *Edward Hays*

or

God of many names and myriad faces, you have inspired countless holy people to a special love of animals. We thank you especially for Saints Gall and Mildburga, patrons of parakeets, finches, and all birds; for Saint Roch, patron of labradors, huskies, and all dogs; Saints George and Martin and Stephen, patrons of mustangs, appaloosas, and all horses; Saint Anthony, patron of cats, hamsters, and all pets; and Saint Francis, patron of fish, rabbits, and all animals. May these and all your holy saints bless the animals assembled here today—with healthy bodies, gentle spirits, and loving hearts. And may the saints bless us too, that we may always be mindful of the needs of our animal companions—and more than that, that we may recognize and cherish them as our greatest friends and as the noblest messengers of your boundless love.

O Saints Gall and Mildburga, pray for our feathered friends.

O Saint Roch, pray for our canine friends.

O Saints George, Martin, and Stephen, pray for our equine friends.

O Saint Anthony, pray for our feline and rodent friends.

O Saint Francis, pray for all our animal friends.

O holy saints of God, pray for us, that we may be loving companions to our animal friends. Amen. *Anthony F. Chiffolo*

If there are but a few pets present, the celebrant, going to each pet and laying his or her hands on the animal, uses the following formulary. If, however, there is a large gathering of pets, the celebrant, in the interest of time, may abbreviate the blessing of each animal by using only the last stanza.

May we, in this holy pattern, now bless _____,
   by taking delight in *his/her* beauty and
   naturalness.
May we bless this animal
   with a Noah-like protection

from all that might harm *him/her*.
May we, like Adam and Eve,
  speak to this creature of Yours
  with kindness and affection,
  reverencing *his/her* life and purpose
  in our communal creation.
May we never treat this creature as a dumb
    animal,
  but rather let us seek to learn its language
  and to be a student of all the secrets
    that it knows.
May Your abundant blessing rest upon
  this creature
  who will be a companion for us in the
  journey of life.
Amen.   *Edward Hays*

When all have been blessed, the celebrant concludes with a final prayer and blessing.

A Prayer Attributed to St. Francis

Lord, make us instruments of your peace. Where there is hatred, let us sow love; where there is injury, pardon; where there is discord, union; where there is doubt, faith; where there is despair, hope; where there is darkness, light; where there is sadness, joy. Grant that we may not so much seek to be consoled as to console; to be understood as to understand; to be loved as to love. For it is in giving that we receive; it is in pardoning that we are pardoned; and it is in dying that we are born to eternal life. Amen.   *traditional*

The Blessing

It was wholly unreasonable to me—this was even before I had gone to school—that in my evening devotions I should pray only for [human beings]. So when my mother had prayed with me and kissed me good night, I used secretly to add another prayer that I had myself composed for all living creatures. It ran like this: "Dear God, guard and bless everything that breathes; keep it from all evil and give it quiet sleep." Amen.

Albert Schweitzer [1875–1965]

At the Closing:
"We Thank You, Lord, For These"
(sung or said)

We thank you, Lord of Heaven, for all the joys
    that greet us,
For all that you have given to help us and delight us
In earth and sky and seas;
The sunlight on the meadows, the rainbow's
    fleeting wonder,
The clouds with cooling shadows, the stars that
    shine in splendor—
We thank you, Lord, for these.

For swift and gallant horses, for lambs and
  pastures springing,
For dogs with friendly faces, for birds with music
  thronging
Their chantries in the trees;
For herbs to cool our fever, for flowers of field
  and garden,
For bees among the clover with stolen sweetness
  laden—
We thank you, Lord, for these.

For homely dwelling places where childhood
  visions linger,
For friendly and kindly voices, for bread to stay
  our hunger
And sleep to bring us ease;
For zeal and zest of living, for faith and
  understanding,
For words to tell our loving, for hope and peace
  unending—
We thank you, Lord, for these.

  Words by Jan Struther [1901–53]; Tune: "Shining Day"

*(If desired, other forms of blessings that appear in this
book may be substituted for those found in this service.)*

The Blessing of the Animals on the Feast of St. Francis of Assisi (October 4)

(Alternative Form—Society of St. Francis, American Province)

Collect

O God, you ever delight to reveal yourself to the childlike and lowly of heart: Grant that, following the example of Francis of Assisi, we may count the wisdom of this world as foolishness and know only Jesus Christ and him crucified; who lives and reigns with you in the unity of the Holy Spirit, one God, for ever and ever. Amen.

First Lesson

The leader of his brothers and the pride of his people was the high priest, Simon son of Onias, who in his life repaired the house, and in his time fortified the temple. He laid the foundations for the high double walls, the high retaining walls for the temple enclosure. In his days a water cistern was dug, a reservoir like the sea in circumference. He considered how to save his people from ruin, and fortified the city against siege. How glorious he was, surrounded by the people, as he came out of the house of the curtain. Like the morning star among the clouds, like the full moon at the festal

season; like the sun shining on the temple of the
Most High, like the rainbow gleaming in splendid
clouds.   *Sirach [Eccl] 50:1–7*

Psalm 37:24–33
(from *Church Service Festivals Office Book*)

(Refrain): Blessed are the poor in spirit,
  for theirs is the dominion of God.

Our steps are directed by you, O God,*
  you strengthen those in whose way you delight.
If they stumble, they shall not fall headlong,*
  for you hold them by the hand.
I have been young and now I am old,*
  but never have I seen the righteous forsaken,
  or their children begging bread. *(Refrain)*
The righteous are always generous in their
    lending,*
  and their children shall be a blessing.
Turn from evil and do good,*
  and dwell in the land for ever.
For you, O God, love justice;*
  you do not forsake your faithful ones. *(Refrain)*
They shall be kept safe for ever,*
  but the offspring of the wicked shall be
    destroyed.
The righteous shall possess the land*
  and dwell in it for ever.
The mouth of the righteous utters wisdom,*

and their tongue speaks what is right.
The law of their God is in their heart,*
   and their footsteps shall not falter. *(Refrain)*

Epistle

May I never boast of anything except the cross of our Lord Jesus Christ, by which the world has been crucified to me, and I to the world. For neither circumcision nor uncircumcision is anything; but a new creation is everything! As for those who will follow this rule—peace be upon them, and mercy, and upon the Israel of God. From now on, let no one make trouble for me; for I carry the marks of Jesus branded on my body. May the grace of our Lord Jesus Christ be with your spirit, brothers and sisters. Amen.   *Gal 6:14–18*

Gospel

Jesus told his disciples, "If any want to become my followers, let them deny themselves and take up their cross and follow me. For those who want to save their life will lose it, and those who lose their life for my sake will find it. For what will it profit them if they gain the whole world but forfeit their life? Or what will they give in return for their life? For the Son of Man is to come with his angels in the glory of his Father, and then he will repay everyone for what has been done."   *Matt 16:24–27*

Prayers of the People

A Litany Based on a Prayer Attributed to St. Francis of Assisi

Leader: With all our heart and all our mind, we pray to you,
O Lord:

People: Make us instruments of your peace.

Leader: For the peace of the world, that a spirit of respect
and forbearance may grow among nations and peoples,
we pray to you, O Lord:

People: Where there is hatred, let us sow love.

Leader: For our enemies and those who wish us harm, and
for all whom we have injured or offended, we pray to
you, O Lord:

People: Where there is injury, let us sow pardon.

Leader: For all who fear God and believe in you, Lord Christ,
that our divisions may cease and all may be one as you
and the Father are one, we pray to you, O Lord:

People: Where there is discord, let us sow union.

Leader: For those who do not yet believe, for those who have
lost their faith, and those in despair and darkness, that
they may receive the light of the Gospel, we pray to you,
O Lord:

People: Where there is doubt, let us sow faith.

Leader: For the poor, the persecuted, the sick and all who
suffer; for refugees, prisoners, and all who are in danger; that they may be relieved and protected, we pray to
you, O Lord:

People: Where there is despair, let us sow hope.

Leader: For the mission of the Church, that in faithful witness

it may preach the Gospel to the ends of the earth, we
pray to you, O Lord:

People: Where there is darkness, let us sow light.

Leader: For those who suffer in body, mind, or spirit; that
they may be comforted and healed; give them courage
and hope in their troubles, and bring them the joy of
your salvation, we pray to you, O Lord:

People: Where there is sadness, let us sow joy.

Other prayers and petitions may be added silently or aloud.
Then all say together:

Grant that we may not so much seek to be consoled, as to
console;
to be understood, as to understand;
to be loved, as to love.

For it is in giving that we receive;
it is in pardoning that we are pardoned;
and it is in dying that we are born to eternal life.

Proper Preface

Because you raised up holy Francis to burn as a
shining light in your Church; that inflamed with
love for God and humankind and the whole of
your creation and bearing in his body the marks of
your Son's passion, he might bring to glory many
sons and daughters:

or

Because you raised up blessed Francis, fired with
love for all that you have made: sun and moon,
earth and wind, fire and water, birds of the air,
sheep and wolves, lepers and beggars:

The Blessing of Pets

Officiant: Grace to you and peace from God our
   Father and from the Lord Jesus Christ.
People: O God, make speed to save us:
   O Lord, make haste to help us.
All: Glory to God, Source of all being,
   Eternal Word and Holy Spirit.
   As it was in the beginning, is now, and will be forever.
   Amen.

The following verses of Psalm 8 may be said in unison:

O God, our Governor
how exalted is your Name in all the world!
What are we that you should be mindful of us?
Your children that you should seek us out?
You have made us but little lower than the angels;
You adorn us with glory and honor.
You give us mastery over the works of your hands;
you put all things under our feet:
All sheep and oxen,
even the wild beasts of the field,
The birds of the air, the fish of the sea,
and whatsoever walks in the paths of the sea.

O God, our Governor
how exalted is your Name in all the world!
Glory to God, Source of all being,
Eternal Word and Holy Spirit
As it was in the beginning, is now, and will be for-
ever. Amen.   *adapted from CSF Office Book*

Officiant: Lord, have mercy.
People: Christ, have mercy.
Officiant: Lord, have mercy.

The Lord's Prayer may be said.
Water may then be blessed.
One or more of the following prayers may be said:

Hear our humble prayer, O God, for our friends the
animals, especially for animals who are suffering,
for any that are hunted or lost or deserted or
frightened or hungry; for all that must be put to
death. We entreat all Thy mercy and pity, and for
those who deal with them we ask a heart of compassion and gentle hands and kindly words. Make
us, ourselves, to be true friends to animals and so
to share the blessings of the merciful.

Albert Schweitzer [1875–1965]

Lord Jesus, King of heaven and earth, Word of the
Father by whom all things were made and given to
us for our use: we humbly ask you to remember us,
your servants. As you give us your help in our

labors and needs, so in your loving kindness bless and protect these animals with your heavenly grace, that we may thankfully praise and glorify your holy Name, who with the Father and the Holy Spirit live and reign, one God, now and forever. Amen.

_____

O merciful Creator, your hand is open wide to satisfy the needs of every living creature: Make us always thankful for your loving providence; and grant that we, remembering the account that we must one day give, may be faithful stewards of your good gifts; through Jesus Christ our Lord. Amen.

The officiant then sprinkles each animal with the blessed water and says:

May this _____ and (s)he who cares for it be blessed in the Name of the Father, and of the Son, and of the Holy Spirit. Amen.

When every animal has been blessed, the officiant dismisses the people:

Officiant: Let us bless the Lord.
People: Thanks be to God.

Hymns Appropriate for St. Francis Day

St. Francis wrote "The Canticle of the Creatures" in 1225. Two versions of this hymn are "All Creatures of Our God and King" and "Most High, Omnipotent Good Lord." Another hymn that shares this theme is "Earth and All Stars."

Although it did not appear until the twentieth century, Francis is often cited as the author of "Lord, Make Us Servants of Your Peace."

Francis had a great devotion to the Passion and is said to have received the marks of the Stigmata—the five wounds of Christ. A hymn that reflects on this and alludes to the epistle is "In the Cross of Christ I Glory."

Francis originated the practice of the Christmas crib at Greccio. An additional verse to "Once in Royal David's City" referencing this event is available at www.societystfrancis.org.

Other appropriate hymns are "Jesu, Jesu"; "Lord, Enthroned in Heavenly Splendor"; "Bread of Heaven, On Thee We Feed"; and "Lift High the Cross."

5

Prayer Services for Remembering or Burying a Pet

Our societies and religions have provided numerous rituals and liturgies to help us grieve the human deaths we experience, but we have no rituals to help us grieve the loss of our beloved animal companions. The loss of a pet is an intense experience and can very often, if not always, be as emotional and distressing as the loss of any human being in our lives. Traditionally, people who have lost their pets have had nowhere to take their grief, no catharsis for their emotional pain, no way to bring closure to their loss. But as it is not a childish or silly thing to mourn a pet, it is quite appropriate to prepare and participate in a service of thanksgiving as a memorial to the wonderful creatures who have brought so much joy to our lives.

Saying Goodbye: A Family's Final Farewell

This service is intended to be used with young children in attendance. It is important that as many members of the family attend as possible, along with pets.

Prior to the service, the family can gather photos, letters, favorite toys, and special memories related to the deceased pet. Making a collage can be a creative activity of remembering: looking through photos and the acts of cutting and pasting are very helpful tools in teaching children to express and accept grief. Creating a flower arrangement would also be a good memorial; the petals of several flowers should be put aside in a bowl or basket for use during the service.

Family members should also be encouraged to write a letter to their pet, or just a few words, to recall some things that made them happy when their pet was with them. This can help children express how they are feeling.

When all have gathered, the remains of the pet are put in their final resting place. A lighted candle, the collage, and favorite toys are placed nearby. A leader, preferably a parent, grandparent, or family elder, acting as the officiant, encourages everyone to hold hands, and then says:

O God, it is time to say goodbye to our pet _____. We loved _____ and we know that _____ loved us. We are glad that _____ is not in any pain. We will miss _____.

Family members then read the letter or words they wrote as a memorial to their pet. When all have had their turn, the leader then asks all to join in saying the Lord's Prayer.

Then each family member in turn takes a small handful of flower petals and lets them fall slowly from their hand over their pet's final resting place, saying, "Go in Peace. Amen." All then bow their heads for a few moments as a silent memorial of thanksgiving.

Finally, the youngest in the group goes to the candle and blows it out. Each family member then says, "Goodbye" *or* "Farewell" *and retires to another place.*

~~≈≈~~

Laid to Rest: The Last Goodbye

This service is designed for any adult who has lost a pet. In preparation, it is important to invite family and friends to be present at the memorial service. Anyone who has ever owned a pet will certainly understand and want to be supportive, and others, if they understand the nature of loss and grieving, will surely make themselves available.

There are many readings from scripture throughout this book that one may choose other than those used below, and this book includes short readings, prayers, and poems that also may be appropriate and helpful. You may choose to lead the service yourself, or preferably, a friend or family member will take on that responsibility. Local clergy may be willing to assist in this way, also.

If it is desirable to have the pet's body or cremains present, they should be placed at the fore of those assembled. Flowers are appropriate and desirable. The closed coffin or container should be covered with a simple cloth.

When all are present, one of the following hymns may be said or sung:

All Creatures of Our God and King

All creatures of our God and King,
lift up your voices, let us sing:
Alleluia, alleluia!
Bright burning sun with golden beams,
pale silver moon that gently gleams,
O praise God, O praise God,
Alleluia, alleluia, alleluia!

Words: Francis of Assisi [1182–1226], trans. by William H. Draper [1855–1933]; Music: "Lasst uns erfreuen," melody from "Auserlesene Catholische Geistliche Kirchengeseng"

All Good Gifts

We plow the fields and scatter the good seed on
the land,
But it is fed and watered by God's almighty hand,
He sends the snow in winter, the warmth to swell
the grain,
the breezes and the sunshine and soft refreshing
rain.

(Refrain) All good gifts around us are sent from
    heaven above;
Then thank the Lord, O thank the Lord for all
    his love.

He only is the Maker of all things near and far;
He paints the wayside flower, he lights the
    evening star;
the winds and waves obey him, by him the birds
    are fed;
much more to us, his children, he gives our daily
    bread.

(Refrain)

We thank thee, then, O Father, for all things
    bright and good,
The seedtime and the harvest, our life, our
    health, our food:
the gifts we have to offer are what thy love
    imparts,
But chiefly thou desirest our humble thankful
    hearts.

(Refrain)

> *Words: Matthais Claudius [1740–1815], trans. by Jane*
> *Montgomery Campbell [1817–78]; Music: "Wir pflugen,"*
> *Johann Abraham Peter Schulz [1747–1800]*

The officiant then says:

Leader: O God, you are the creator of all things.

People: In you we live and move and have our being.

Leader: Let us pray. We thank you, God, that you have brought us together, to this one place, to say our farewells to one of the many wonderful creatures you have given us as companions to share our lives. We pray now that _____, faithful companion, may know your peace. And we ask your blessing and presence for all who mourn, that casting all our grief on you, they may be comforted. All this we ask in your name. Amen.

A reading from scripture then follows, or a poem, or both.

A Reading from Ecclesiastes (3:18–21)

I said in my heart with regard to human beings that God is testing them to show that they are but animals. For the fate of humans and the fate of animals is the same; as one dies, so dies the other. They all have the same breath, and humans have no advantage over the animals.... All go to one place; all are from the dust, and all turn to dust again. Who knows whether the human spirit goes upward and the spirit of animals goes downward to the earth?

or

A Reading from Job (12:7–10)

"But ask the animals, and they will teach you;
   the birds of the air, and they will tell you;
ask the plants of the earth, and they will teach you;
   and the fish of the sea will declare to you.
Who among all these does not know
   that the hand of the Lord has done this?
In his hand is the life of every living thing
   and the breath of every human being."

or

A Reading from "For Katrina's Sundial"

Time is
Too slow for those who wait,
Too swift for those who fear,
Too long for those who grieve,
Too short for those who rejoice.
But for those who love,
Time is eternity.   *Henry van Dyke [1852–1933]*

*Following the readings, a minister, if present, may preach
a homily. If no minister is present, those in attendance may
express words of remembrance, words of comfort, and a tribute
to the deceased pet. The speakers may want to focus on the
themes of joyful memories, a happy issue out of all afflictions,
and a reasonable and holy hope for the future.*

When all have finished, the leader then says the following prayer, adapted from the writings of William Penn (1644–1718):

We seem to give _____ back to you, dear God, who gave _____ to us. Yet as you did not lose _____ in giving, so we have not lost _____ by *his/her* return. Not as the world gives do you give, O lover of souls. For what is yours is ours always if we are yours. And life is eternal, and love is immortal; and death is only a horizon, and a horizon is nothing more than the limit of our sight. Amen.

The officiant then leads those assembled in the Lord's Prayer. Then follows the Committal, when the remains of the deceased pet are taken to or placed in their final resting place. Once all is in place, then is sung or said the following hymn:

Lord, make us servants of your peace: where there
    is hate, may we sow love;
where there is hurt, may we forgive; where there is
    strife, may we make one.

Where all is doubt, may we sow faith; where all is
    gloom, may we sow hope;
where all is night, may we sow light; where all is
    tears, may we sow joy.

Jesus, our Lord, may we not seek to be consoled,
    but to console,

nor look to understanding hearts, but look for
hearts to understand.

May we not look for love's return, but seek to love
unselfishly,
for in our giving we receive, and in forgiving are
forgiven.

Dying, we live, and are reborn through death's
dark night to endless day:
Lord, make us servants of your peace, to wake at
last in heaven's light.

Words: James Quinn, based on prayer att. to Francis of
Assisi [1182–1226]; Music: "Dickinson College,"
Lee Hastings Bristol, Jr. [1923–79]

All present then take roses or some other flowers, or petals
from a flower, and individually place them on top of or beside
the coffin or urn, saying, "Go in peace."

The officiant then reads a final verse from "Now the
Green Blade Riseth":

When our hearts are wintry, grieving or in pain,
thy touch can call us back to life again,
field of our hearts that dead and bare have been,
Love is come again like wheat that springeth
green.

Words: John Macleod Campbell Crum [1872–1958];
Music: "Noël nouvelet," medieval French carol

The officiant then asks God's blessing for all God's creatures:

O Creator of the Universe, we ask your blessings on all who stand here today before you humbled by the grave and gate of death. Pour upon us your love and give us insight into your will for the world. Lift us up in our sorrow with the knowledge that love is immortal, and that all good things come to those who wait patiently in faith. Guard us, guide us, and keep us on the path of companionship, obedience, loyalty, and a zeal for life that the animals who are our companions have taught us. May the gifts they have so freely given us be given to them as they live on in our memories eternally. Amen.

The people depart in silence; or if a final hymn is desired, then the following may be said or sung:

Let All Things Now Living
(sung to the melody of "The Ash Grove")

Let all things now living a song of thanksgiving
To God the creator triumphantly raise.
Who fashioned and made us, protected and stayed
    us,
Who still guides us on to the end of our days.
God's banners are o'er us, his light goes before us,
A pillar of fire shining forth in the night.
Till shadows have vanished and darkness is
    banished

As forward we travel from light into light.
His law he enforces, the stars in their courses
And sun in its orbit obediently shine;
The hills and the mountains, the rivers and
  fountains,
The deeps of the ocean proclaim him divine.
We too should be voicing our love and rejoicing;
With glad adoration a Song let us raise
Till all things now living unite in thanksgiving:
"To God in the highest, Hosanna and praise!"

Words: Katherine K. Davis [1892–1980];

Music: traditional Welsh melody

Lighting a Memorial Candle

To keep beloved pets alive in the memory, a family may hold a short memorial ceremony, on the anniversary of their death, their birth, or some other special occasion.

To begin, the family can arrange a few treasured photos (or paintings/drawings) of the pet in a special place, either inside or out, along with a commemorative candle. A small flower arrangement may also be appropriate.

When all the members of the family have gathered together, the candle is lit, and the following prayer is recited:

Merciful God, we turn to you in prayer at this time
of remembrance. The link of life that bound us to
_____ has been broken, but feelings of love continue to bind us together. We give thanks for the
gift of _____'s life, companionship, and memory.
Help us understand how our lives have been formed
and shaped by what _____ was and did...
  May *his/her* memory be a blessing.
  As long as we live, they too will live, for they are
part of us as long as we remember them.

adapted from Kol Haneshamah:
Songs, Blessings and Rituals for the Home

*The assembled family may then recite a prayer or poem
appropriate to the pet's memory. When all have had a chance
to share their thoughts, the following prayer for all creatures of
God is recited:*

We give them back to you, dear Lord,
Who gave them to us.
Yet as you did not lose them in giving,
So we have not lost them by their return.
For what is yours is ours always, if we are yours.
And life is eternal and love is immortal,
And death is only a horizon,
And a horizon is nothing more
Than the limit of our sight.

Quaker prayer, adapted from the writings of
William Penn [1644–1718]

The candle is then extinguished as the assembled family quietly disperses.

Planting a Memorial Tree

Over the course of recent decades, the Jewish people have developed a practice of planting a memorial tree in memory of loved ones who have died. In addition to the planting of a new tree, the ritual includes telling the life story of the beloved whom the tree commemorates and reciting prayers of mourning. Some families might find that planting a tree in memory of a pet who has died helps bring healing to their sorrowing hearts.

Before the ceremony, the family should have obtained the tree and should have selected the location where it will be planted. At the site, perhaps on a small table, special photos (or paintings/drawings) of the pet should be arranged, along with a commemorative candle. A small flower arrangement might also be appropriate. Someone should already have excavated the hole for the tree, which should be ready for planting.

At the appointed time, the family assembles at the site. As the candle is lit, the following prayer is recited:

Merciful God, we turn to you in prayer at this time of remembrance. The link of life that bound us to _____ has been broken, but feelings of love continue to bind us together. We give thanks for the gift of _____'s life, companionship, and memory. Help us understand how our lives have been formed and shaped by what _____ was and did...

May *his/her* memory be a blessing.

As long as we live, they too will live, for they are part of us as long as we remember them.

adapted from Kol Haneshamah:
Songs, Blessings and Rituals for the Home

The assembled family then shares their memories of their beloved pet. As well, family members may recite a prayer or poem appropriate to the pet's memory. When all have had a chance to share their thoughts, the following prayer is recited:

Almighty God, my soul is full of agony. You have taken one I loved from my eyes and I have no one to help me. My heart is desolate. Please comfort me, for I am in great trouble.

Teach me, O God, in this hour of sorrow, in this great bereavement, on this most bitter day, to have patience and God-like resignation. Teach me to follow your will with meekness as well as strength. You know my sorrows and my tears. Look upon me and give me help. Enable me to bear the weight of this trial, for I am unable to bear it alone. Pity me,

good Lord; pity me, gracious God; turn your face
toward me and mercifully accept my prayer. Amen.

adapted from a traditional prayer

*The hole for the tree is then watered and the tree is
placed in the ground. Then all family members in turn place
a handful of dirt upon the tree's roots. As one person then fin-
ishes placing the soil around the tree, the rest of the family
recites one of the following prayers:*

You would know the secret of death.
But how shall you find it unless you seek it in the
    heart of life?
The owl whose night-bound eyes are blind unto
    the day cannot unveil the mystery of light.
If you would indeed behold the spirit of death,
    open your heart wide unto the body of life.
For life and death are one, even as the river and
    the sea are one.
In the depth of your hopes and desires lies your
    silent knowledge of the beyond; And like seeds
    dreaming beneath the snow, your heart dreams
    of spring.
Trust the dreams, for in them is hidden the gate to
    eternity.   *Kahlil Gibran [1883–1931]*, The Prophet

or

You grieve where no grief is necessary.
The wise-hearted mourn neither for the living
Nor for the dead.

You and I and all who have
Come to be here have always been
And will never cease to be.

Beyond birth and death are the spirit.
Death does not touch it,
Though the house of the spirit seems to die.

The end of birth is death;
The end of death is birth.
As it is so ordained,
What is there to bring sorrow?

from a traditional Hindu story

The candle is then extinguished as the assembled family quietly disperses.

6

Additional Prayers, Hymns, Poems, and Readings

When a loved one dies, there are no words sufficient to express the grief we feel. Yet we all sense how important it is to offer words of condolence, if not to ourselves, then to others who are grieving. In our time of searching for meaning in the midst of sorrow, it is a comfort to know that many persons long before us thought about, prayed, sang, and wrote beautiful verses or remembrances to honor their pets—their love and their lives. For those who don't know quite what to say, or where to look to begin the process of healing, we have gathered some of the best of centuries of thought about animals and the special ways in which they touch our lives.

On Death

For everything there is a season, and a time for
    every matter under heaven:
    a time to be born, and a time to die…

Eccl 3:1–2

Set me as a seal upon your heart,
    as a seal upon your arm;
for love is strong as death,
    passion fierce as the grave.
Its flashes are flashes of fire,
    a raging flame.
Many waters cannot quench love,
    neither can floods drown it.
If one offered for love
    all the wealth of his house,
    it would be utterly scorned.

Song 8:6–7

I am that living and fiery Essence of the divine sub-
stance that glows in the beauty of the fields. I shine
in the water, I burn in the sun, and the moon, and
the stars. Mine is the mysterious force of the invis-
ible wind. I permeate all things, that they may not
die. I am Life.   *Hildegard of Bingen [1098–1179]*

They that love beyond the world cannot be sepa-
rated by it. Death is but crossing the world, as

friends do the seas; they live in one another still.

William Penn [1644–1718]

But true love is a durable fire,
 In the mind ever burning,
Never sick, never old, never dead,
 From itself never turning.

Sir Walter Raleigh [c. 1552–1618]

The grave itself is but a
 covered bridge
Leading from light to light,
 through a brief darkness.

Henry Wadsworth Longfellow [1807–82]

Everything that lives, lives not alone nor for itself.

William Blake [1757–1827]

Nothing is ever really lost, or can be lost,
No birth, identity, form—no object of the world,
Nor life, nor force, nor any visible thing;
Appearance must not foil, nor shifted sphere
 confuse thy brain.
Ample are time and space—ample the fields of
 Nature.   *Walt Whitman [1819–92]*

Passing Away

Passing away, saith the World, passing away:
Chances, beauty and youth sapp'd day by day:
Thy life never continueth in one stay.

Is the eye waxen dim, is the dark hair changing to
  gray
That hath won neither laurel nor bay?
I shall clothe myself in Spring and bud in May:
Thou, root-stricken, shalt not rebuild thy decay
On my bosom for aye.
Then I answer'd: Yea.

Passing away, saith my Soul, passing away:
With its burden of fear and hope, of labour and
  play,
Hearken what the past doth witness and say:
Rust in thy gold, a moth is in thine array,
A canker is in thy bud, thy leaf must decay.
At midnight, at cockcrow, at morning, one certain
  day,
Lo, the Bridegroom shall come and shall not
  delay:
Watch thou and pray.
Then I answer'd: Yea.

Passing away, saith my God, passing away:
Winter passeth after the long delay:
New grapes on the vine, new figs on the tender
  spray,
Turtle calleth turtle in Heaven's May.
Though I tarry, wait for me, trust me, watch and
  pray.
Arise, come away; night is past, and lo, it is day;

My love, my sister, my spouse, thou shalt hear me
  say—
Then I answer'd: Yea.   *Christina Rossetti [1830–94]*

Death a Quiet Door
Death is only an old door
Set in a garden wall;
On gentle hinges it gives, at dusk
When the thrushes call.

Along the lintel are green leaves,
Beyond the light lies still;
Very willing and weary feet
Go over that sill.

There is nothing to trouble any heart;
Nothing to hurt at all.
Death is only a quiet door
In an old wall.   *Nancy Byrd Turner [1880–1954]*

Death is nothing at all—I have only slipped away
into the next room. Whatever we were to each
other, that we are still. Call me by my old familiar
name. Speak to me in the easy way we always used.
I am but waiting for you, for an interval, somewhere
very near, just around the corner. All is well.
Nothing is passed. Nothing is lost. One brief
moment, and all will be as it was before, only better,
happier, and forever.   *Henry Scott Holland [1847–1918]*

The Bustle in a House
The Morning after Death
Is solemnest of industries
Enacted upon Earth—

The Sweeping up the Heart
And putting Love away
We shall not want to use again
Until Eternity. *Emily Dickinson [1830–86]*

Warm summer sun, shine kindly here;
Warm western wind, blow softly here;
Green sod above, lie light, lie light—
Good-night, dear heart, good-night, good-night.

Robert Richardson [1850–1901],
adapted by Mark Twain [1835–1910]

Strange is our situation here upon earth. Each of
us comes for a short visit, not knowing why, yet
sometimes seeming to divine a purpose. From the
standpoint of daily life, however, there is one thing
we do know: That we are here for the sake of others…. Above all, for those upon whose smile and
well-being our own happiness depends, and also
for the countless unknown souls with whose fate
we are connected by a bond of sympathy.

Albert Einstein [1879–1955]

Next to the encounter of death in our own bodies,
the most sensible calamity to an honest man is the

death of a friend. The comfort of having a friend
may be taken away, but not that of having had one.
Shall a man bury his friendship with his friend?

Seneca [4 B.C.E.–C.E. 65]

That time of year thou mayst in me behold,
When yellow leaves, or none, or few do hang
Upon those boughs which shake against the cold,
Bare ruined choirs, where late the sweet birds
  sang.
In me thou seest the twilight of such day,
As after sunset fadeth in the west,
Which by and by black night doth take away,
Death's second self that seals up all in rest.
In me thou seest the glowing of such fire,
That on the ashes of his youth doth lie,
As the death-bed, whereon it must expire,
Consumed with that which it was nourished by.
  This thou perceiv'st, which makes thy love
      more strong,
  To love that well, which thou must leave ere
      long.   *William Shakespeare [1564–1616]*

Request from the Rainbow Bridge
Weep not for me though I am gone
Into that gentle night.
Grieve if you will, but not for long
Upon my soul's sweet flight.
I am at peace, my soul's at rest,
There is no need for tears.

For with your love I was so blessed
For all those many years.
There is no pain, I suffer not,
The fear now all is gone.
Put now these things out of your thoughts.
In your memory I live on.
Remember not my fight for breath,
Remember not the strife.
Please do not dwell upon my death,
But celebrate my life.   *Constance Jenkins*

The Grave
'Tis but a night, a long and moonless night,
We make the Grave our bed, and then are gone.
Thus at the shut of ev'n, the weary bird
Leaves the wide air, and in some lonely brake
Cow'rs down, and dozes till the dawn of day,
Then claps his well-fledg'd wings, and bears away.
                              Robert Blair [1699–1746]

At this grief my heart was utterly darkened; and
whatever I beheld was death. My native country
was a torment to me, and my father's house a
strange unhappiness; and whatever I had shared
with him, wanting him, became a distracting torture. Mine eyes sought him everywhere, but he
was not granted them; and I hated all places, for
that they had not him; nor could they now tell
me, "he is coming," as when he was alive and
absent. I became a great riddle to myself, and I

asked my soul, why she was so sad, and why she disquieted me sorely: but she knew not what to answer me....

Thus was I wretched, and that wretched life I held dearer than my friend...for at once I loathed exceedingly to live, and feared to die. I suppose, the more I loved him, the more did I hate, and fear (as a most cruel enemy) death, which had bereaved me of him: and I imagined it would speedily make an end of all...since it had power over him...I felt that my soul and his soul were "one soul in two bodies": and therefore was my life a horror to me, because I would not live halved. And therefore perchance I feared to die, lest he whom I had much loved, should die wholly.

St. Augustine [354–430]

Let your weeping be bitter and your wailing
    fervent;
  make your mourning worthy of the departed,
for one day, or two, to avoid criticism;
  then be comforted for your grief.
For grief may result in death,
  and a sorrowful heart saps one's strength....
Do not give your heart to grief;
  drive it away, and remember your own end.
Do not forget, there is no coming back;
  you do the dead no good, and you injure
    yourself.

Remember his fate, for yours is like it;
yesterday it was his, and today it is yours.
When the dead is at rest, let his remembrance
rest too,
and be comforted for him when his spirit has
departed.   *Sirach [Eccl] 38:17–23*

Ascension Hymn
Dear, beauteous death! the Jewel of the Just,
Shining no where, but in the dark;
What mysteries do lie beyond thy dust,
Could man outlook that mark!

He that hath found some fledg'd bird's nest, may
know
At first sight, if the bird be flown;
But what fair Well, or Grove he sings in now,
That is to him unknown.

And yet, as Angels in some brighter dreams
Call to the soul, when man doth sleep:
So some strange thoughts transcend our wonted
themes,
And into glory peep....
                    Henry Vaughan [c. 1622–95]

Untitled
And now we lay you down to sleep
You're finally at rest
Our love for you we'll always keep
You were the very best

You gave us joy for all these years
A memory for each new day

Then came the day of all my fears
The day you passed away

A part of us you took with you
And I can't stand the pain

But when this life on earth is through
I know we'll meet again.   *author unknown*

On the Death of Animals

It is natural to grieve; it is the loss of that which is love. Again and again, scripture reminds us that God grieved and still grieves for that which is created when it is no longer truly alive. So it is not only natural but right that, created in God's image, we too grieve when life is lost, any life—all life. It is natural and right to grieve over the loss of a pet that we loved, as God loves. Would the God of love expect anything less of us? I think not.

There are those who ask the question, "Do animals have souls like ours, and will they be with us in an afterlife?" In a loss situation this question is best heard as an expression of the deep love for that which is lost in death. It is not so important to search for the answer to that which only God knows, as to trust that which God loves is always under God's care. We, as a people of faith, are our own proof of this comforting truth.

[The Rev.] Canon Joel A. Gibson, former subdean,
The Cathedral Church of St. John the Divine, New York City

Animals are such agreeable friends—
  they ask no questions,
  they pass no criticisms.

George Eliot [1819–80]

We need another and wiser and perhaps more mystical concept of animals. We patronize them for their incompleteness, for their tragic fate of having taken form so far below ourselves. And therein we err, and greatly err. For the animal shall not be measured by man. In a world older and more complete than ours they move finished and complete, gifted with extensions of the senses we have lost or never attained, living by voices we shall never hear. They are not brethren; they are not underlings; they are other nations, caught with ourselves in the nest of life and time, fellow prisoners of the splendour and the travail ahead.

Henry Beston [1888–1968]

If I spent enough time with the tiniest creature—even a caterpillar—I would never have to prepare a sermon. So full of God is every creature.

Meister Eckhart [1260–1327]

Let me never forget that the same God who made
me, made the whole world and all animals that are
in it.   *John Cardinal Newman [1801–90]*

I am the self abiding
in the heart of all creatures;
I am their beginning,
their middle and their end.
Know that my brilliance,
flaming in the sun,
in the moon, and in fire,
illumines this whole universe.   *Bhagavad-Gita*

There is not a beast on earth, nor fowl that flieth
on two wings, but they are a people like unto you,
and to God they shall return.   *The Koran*

One should pay attention to even the smallest
crawling creature, for these too may have a valu-
able lesson to teach us, and even the smallest ant
may wish to communicate with man.

Black Elk [1863–1950]

We should understand well that all things are the
work of the Great Spirit. We should know the Great
Spirit is within all things: the trees, the grasses, the
rivers, the mountains, and the four-legged and
winged peoples; and even more important, we
should understand that the Great Spirit is also
above all these things and peoples. When we do

understand all this deeply in our hearts, then we
will fear, and love, and know the Great Spirit, and
then we will be and act and live as the Spirit
intends.   *Black Elk [1863–1950]*

Song of Myself
I think I could turn and live with animals,
They are so placid and self-contain'd.
I stand and look at them long and long.
They do not lie awake in the dark and weep for
   their sins,
They do not make me sick discussing their duty to
   God;
Not one is dissatisfied, not one is demented with
   the mania of owning things,
Not one kneels to another, nor to his kind that
   lived thousands of years ago,
Not one is respectable or unhappy over the whole
   earth.   *Walt Whitman [1819–92]*

O Lord, how manifold are your works!
   In wisdom you have made them all;
   the earth is full of your creatures....

These all look to you,
   to give them their food in due season;
when you give it to them, they gather it up;
   when you open your hand, they are filled with
      good things.

When you hide your face, they are dismayed;
    when you take away their breath, they die
    and return to their dust.
When you send forth your spirit, they are created;
    and you renew the face of the ground.

May the glory of the Lord endure forever;
    may the Lord rejoice in his works....

                     Ps 104:24, 27–31

————————

Know, first, that heaven, and earth's compacted
    frame,
And flowing waters, and the starry frame,
And both the radiant lights, one common soul
Inspires and feeds—and animates the whole.
This active mind, infused through all space,
Unites and mingles with the mighty mass:
Hence, men and beasts the breath of life obtain,
And birds of air, and monsters of the main.
Th'ethereal vigour is in all the same,
And every soul is filled with equal flame.

                     Virgil [70–19 B.C.E.]

————————

He prayeth well who loveth well both man and
bird and beast.   *Samuel Taylor Coleridge [1772– 1834]*

————————

I look up to the sky and the stars,
And down to the earth and the things that creep
    there,

And I consider in my heart how their creation
Was planned with wisdom in every detail.

Shmuel Hanagid [993–1056]

The insect in the plant, the moth which spends its
brief hours of existence hovering about the candle's
flame—nay, the life which inhabits a drop of water,
is as much an object of God's special providence as
the mightiest monarch on his throne.

Henry Bergh [1811–88], founder, ASPCA

The wolf shall live with the lamb,
  the leopard shall lie down with the kid.
the calf and the lion and the fatling together,
  and a little child shall lead them.
The cow and the bear shall graze,
  their young shall lie down together;
  and the lion shall eat straw like the ox.

Isa 11:6–7

How wonderful, O God, are the works of your
hands! The heavens declare your glory, the arch of
sky displays your handiwork.

In your love you have given us the power to behold
the beauty of your world, robed in all its splendor.
The sun and the stars, the valleys and hills, the
rivers and lakes—all disclose your presence.

The roaring breakers of the sea tell of your awesome
might; the beasts of the field and the birds of the

air bespeak your wondrous will. All life comes
forth by your creative will.

In your goodness you have made us able to hear
the music of the world. The raging of the winds,
the whispering of trees in the wood, the precious
voices of all created life reveal to us that you are in
our midst. A divine voice sings through all creation.   *Rabbi Harold S. White, International Network*
                                    for Religion and Animals

Of all created things the source is one,
Simple, single as love; remember
The cell and seed of life, the sphere
That is, of child, white bird, and small blue
     dragonfly,
Green fern and the gold four-petaled tormentilla
The ultimate memory.
Each latent cell puts out a future,
Unfolds its differing complexity
As a tree puts forth leaves, and spins a fate
Fern-traced, bird-feathered, or fish-scaled.
Moss spreads its green film on the moist peat,
The germ of dragonfly pulses into animation
     and takes wing
As the water lily from the mud ascends on its
     ropy stem
To open a sweet white calyx to the sky.
Open our eyes, God, to all of these marvels.

May we proclaim with the Psalmist:
"This is the day which God has made. Let us
   rejoice and be glad thereon."

Rabbi Harold S. White, International Network
for Religion and Animals

The Peace of Wild Things
When despair for the world grows in me
and I wake in the night at the least sound
in fear of what my life and my children's lives may
   be,
I go and lie down where the wood drake
rests in his beauty on the water, and the great
   heron feeds.
I come into the peace of wild things
who do not tax their lives with forethought
of grief. I come into the presence of still water.
And I feel above me the day-blind stars
waiting with their light. For a time
I rest in the grace of the world, and am free.

Wendell Berry

For Cats

The Difference between Dogs and Cats
A dog thinks: Hey, these people I live with feed
me, love me, provide me with a nice warm, dry
house, pet me, and take good care of me...they
must be Gods!

A cat thinks: Hey, these people I live with feed me, love me, provide me with a nice warm, dry house, pet me, and take good care of me...I must be a God!   *author unknown*

No heaven will not ever heaven be
Unless my cats are there to welcome me.

Mark Twain [1835–1910]

The cat has too much spirit to have no heart...

Mark Twain [1835–1910]

If a man were to be crossed with a cat, it would improve the man but deteriorate the cat.

Mark Twain [1835–1910]

Adam said, "Lord, when I was in the garden, you walked with me every day. Now I do not see you anymore. I am lonesome here, and it is difficult for me to remember how much you love me." This was before God created Eve.

And God said, "No problem! I will create a companion for you who will be with you forever and who will be a reflection of my love for you, so that you will love me even when you cannot see me. Regardless of how selfish or childish or unlovable you may be, this new companion will accept you as you are and will love you as I do, in spite of yourself."

And God created a new animal to be a companion for Adam. And it was a good animal. And God was pleased. And the new animal was pleased to be with Adam and wagged its tail.

And Adam said, "Lord, I have already named all the animals in the kingdom, and I cannot think of a name for this new animal."

And God said, "No problem! Because I have created this new animal to be a reflection of my love for you, its name will be a reflection of my own name, and you will call it Dog."

And Dog lived with Adam and was a companion to him and loved him. And Adam was comforted. And God was pleased. And Dog was content and wagged its tail.

After a while, it came to pass that Adam's guardian angel came to the Lord and said, "Lord, Adam has become filled with pride. He struts and preens like a peacock, and he believes he is worthy of adoration. Dog has indeed taught him that he is loved, but perhaps too well."

And God said, "No problem! I will create for him a companion who will be with him forever and who will see him as he is. The companion will remind him of his limitations, so he will know that he is not always worthy of adoration."

And God created Cat to be a companion to Adam.

And Cat would not obey Adam. And when Adam gazed into Cat's eyes, he was reminded that he was not the supreme being. And Adam learned humility.

And God was pleased. And Adam was greatly improved. And Dog was happy. And Cat didn't give a damn one way or another.   *author unknown*

Cats, no less liquid than their shadows,
Offer no angles to the wind.
They slip, diminished, neat, through loopholes,
Less than themselves.   *A. S. J. Tessimond [1902–62]*

A cat pours his body on the floor like water. It is restful just to see him.

     William Lyon Phelps [1865–1943]

I believe cats to be spirits come to earth. A cat, I am sure, could walk on a cloud without coming through.   *Jules Verne [1828–1905]*

Cats are intended to teach us that not everything in life has a function.   *Garrison Keillor*

If a fish is the movement of water embodied, given shape, then a cat is a diagram and pattern of subtle air.   *Doris Lessing*

Stray
For I will consider my Cat, Red Dog,
So named of the Following Categories: Red and
     Dog.
For he was born Red of fur and disposition.

For though not a Dog, he disporteth himself as
   One.
And trifling as paw to yarn, and loyal as tongue
   to tunafish,
He is mine as much as he is not,
That is, he belongeth to the grass, as I do,
And to the stream of air.
When taking it in or weaving through it, his
   shoulder blades
rut the breeze as plowshares.
And he belongeth to the General Category of Lost,
   as I do.

For Red Dog, he did wander by
but he did wander away.

We thought there'd be a prophecy, or at least
a bulletin, mimeographed and hung
child-high on trees. Why no random heralds
for Him who came at Random, blown like litter,
caterwauling? Thus we looked for signs,
though found we none. A universe obstinate
and ambiguous, our moral noses not keen,
we feared to keep him. We let stray be stray.

For Red Dog, he did wander by
and he did wander away.

The last time I saw Red Dog, that very day
There did arrive a bottle-fly blue pick-up truck,
Specific Category Hot Rod,

Abundant in cubic inches enough to crush a cat,
Wheels doubled up & high, very clean, Large
   & Category Invention
Driver drifting over the purr, thoughts of Personal
   Recreation Devices,
Slapper of aftershave, ears full of Heavy Metal,
   Red Neck,
a brother of cats under his skin.

Let stray be stray, you counseled me, smell of her
   cutting your beard.

And Red Dog, he did wander by
but he did wander away.

An errant driver in his big cat came,
post hoc, ergo propter hoc you vanished
   Fallaciously.
This much I know, who has no proof, no body.
Only the stroking feel of conviction about my
   ankle,
I occupy the Sidelong Category Disposed Of,
   and Red Dog too,
With Stung, a chapped pink cheek,
And absence, that Saucy Knave,
   that hot salt.   *Julie Sheehan*

———————

We have learned many things from living with [our
cats]. Some lessons are directives we would be
wise to follow: Live a rhythmic life. Sit and savor

the present moment. Gaze intently. Stretch often. Keep out of harm's way. Take good care of your family. Be independent, but don't be afraid of being dependent on others. Cherish your wildness, even if no one else does. When you want something, be persistent. When someone pays attention to you, respond with affection. If you are embarrassed, turn your back on the situation and get on with your life. Enjoy small treats. Keep yourself clean. Take a nap when you need one, and try to relax more. *Frederic and Mary Ann Brussat*

In Islam, cats rank far above dogs. The Prophet prescribed that cats should be well treated, since they protected the tents of nomads from snakes. In Tunis, these animals are thought to have souls, and to be true Muslims facing Mecca when they perform their ablutions. *author unknown*

The smallest feline is a masterpiece. *Leonardo da Vinci [1452–1519]*

To a Cat
Stately, kindly, lordly friend,
   Condescend
Here to sit by me, and turn
Glorious eyes that smile and burn,
Golden eyes,
Love's lustrous meed,
On the golden page I read.

All your wondrous wealth of hair,
  Dark and fair,
Silken-shaggy, soft and bright
As the clouds and beams of night,
Pays my reverent hand's caress
Back with friendlier gentleness.

Dogs may fawn on all, and some
  As they come;
You, a friend of loftier mind,
Answer friends along in kind;
Just your foot upon my hand
Softly bids it understand....

Wild on woodland ways, your sires
  Flashed like fires;
Fair as flame, and fierce, and fleet,
As with wings and wingless feet,
Shone and sprang your mother, free,
Bright and brave as wind or sea.

Free, and proud, and glad as they,
  Here today
Rests or roams their radiant child,
Vanquished not, but reconciled;
Free from curb of aught above
Save the lovely curb of love.

Love, through dreams of souls divine,
  Fain would shine

'Round a dawn whose light and song
Then should right our mutual wrong.—
Speak, and seal the love-lit law,
Sweet Assisi's seer foresaw.

Dreams were theirs; yet happily may
   Dawn a day
When such friends and fellows born,
Seeing our earth as fair at morn,
May, for wiser love's sake, see
More of heaven's deep heart than we.

Algernon Charles Swinburne [1837–1909]

The Kitten
And yet, for thou hast, I ween,
So oft our favoured playmate been,
Soft be the change which thou shalt prove
When time hath spoiled thee of our love;
Still be thou deemed by housewife fat,
A comely, careful, mousing cat,
Whose dish is, for the public good,
Replenished oft with savoury food.
Nor, when thy span of life be past,
Be thou to pond or dunghill cast;
But gently born on good man's spade,
Beneath the decent sod be laid.
And children show with glistening eyes,
The place where poor old cat he lies.

Joanna Baillie [1762–1851]

With the qualities of cleanliness, affection, patience, dignity, and courage that cats have, how many of us, I ask you, would be capable of becoming cats?
Fernand Méry [1887–1984]

God made the cat in order that man might have the pleasure of caressing the lion.
Fernand Méry [1887–1984]

A dog is a dog, a bird is a bird, and a cat is a person.
attributed to Mugsy Peabody

I love cats because I enjoy my home; and little by little, they become its visible soul.
Jean Cocteau [1889–1963]

A kitten is the rosebud in the garden of the animal kingdom.
Robert Southey [1774–1843]

A Cat
Silently licking his gold-white paw,
Oh gorgeous Celestino, for
God made lovely things, yet
Our lovely cat surpasses them all;
The gold, the iron, the waterfall,
The nut, the peach, apple, granite
Are lovely things to look at, yet,
Our lovely cat surpasses them all.
John Gittings, age 8

The Little Cat Angel
The ghost of a little white kitten
Crying mournfully, early and late,
Distracted St. Peter, the watchman,
As he guarded the heavenly gate.
"Say, what do you mean," said his saintship,
"Coming here and behaving like that?"
"I want to see Nellie, my missus,"
Sobbed the wee little ghost of a cat.
"I know she's not happy without me,
Won't you open and let me go in?"
"Begone," gasped the horrified watchman,
"Why the very idea is a sin;
I open the gate to good angels,
Not to stray little beggars like you."
"All right," mewed the little white kitten,
"Though a cat I'm a good angel, too."
Amazed at so bold an assertion,
But aware that he must make no mistake,
In silence, St. Peter long pondered,
For his name and repute were at stake.
Then placing the cat in his bosom
With a "Whist now, and say all your prayers,"
He opened the heavenly portals
And ascended the bright golden stairs.
A little girl angel came flying,
"That's my kitty, St. Peter," she cried.
And, seeing the joy of their meeting,
Peter let the cat angel abide.

This tale is the tale of a kitten
Dwelling now with the blessed above,
It vanquished grim Death and High Heaven
For the name of the kitten was Love.

Leontine Stanfield [b.1866, Claribel Leontine]

In Memoriam—Leo: A Yellow Cat
If to your twilight land of dream—
    Persephone, Persephone,
Drifting with all your shadow host—
Dim sunlight comes, with sudden gleam
And you lift veilèd eyes to see
Slip past a little golden ghost,
That wakes a sense of springing flowers,
Of nesting birds, and lambs newborn,
Of spring astir in quickening hours,
And young blades of Demeter's corn;
For joy of that sweet glimpse of sun,
O Goddess of unnumbered dead,
Give one soft touch—if only one—
To that uplifted, pleading head!
Whisper some kindly word, to bless
A wistful soul who understands
That life is but one long caress
Of gentle words and gentle hands.

Margaret Pollock Sherwood [1864–1955]

Leo to His Mistress
   (Answer)
Dear Mistress, do not grieve for me
Even in such sweet poetry.
Alas! It is too late for that,
No mistress can recall her cat.
Eurydice remained a shade
Despite the music Orpheus played;
And pleasures here outlast, I guess,
Your earthly transitoriness.

You serious denizens of Earth
Know nothing of Elysian mirth;
With other shades I play or doze
And wash, and stretch, or rub my nose.
I hunt for mice, or take a nap
Safe in Iphigenia's lap.
At times I bite Achilles' heel
To learn if shadow heroes squeal,
And should he turn to do me hurt,
I hide beneath Cassandra's skirt.

But should he smile, no creature bolder,
I lightly bounce upon his shoulder,
Then leap to fair Electra's knee
Or scamper with Antigone.
I chase the rolling woolen ball
Penelope has just let fall,
And crouch when Meleager's cheer
Awakes the shades of trembling deer.

I grin when Stygian boys, beguiled,
Stare after Helen, Ruin's child;
Or should these placid pastimes fail
I play with Cerberus's tail.
At last I purr and spit and spatter
When kind Demeter fills my platter.

And yet, in spite of all this,
I sometimes yearn for earthly bliss,
To hear you calling "Leo!" when
The glorious sun awakens men;
Or hear your "Good night, Pussy" sound
When starlight falls on mortal ground;
Then, in my struggles to get free,
I almost scratch Persephone.

Henry Dwight Sedgwick [1861–1957]

...a family cat is not replaceable like a worn-out coat or a set of tires. Each new kitten becomes his own cat, and none is repeated. I am four-cats old, measuring out my life in friends that have succeeded, but not replaced one another.   *Irving Townsend [1920–81]*

The cat is eloquent of home. The cat is the companion of the fireside. The cat is the banisher of pessimism, the comforter of loneliness and the humbler of false pride. The cares of the day may be heavy, the problems of living may oppress and discourage, but come home from them in the evening, sit down with the family cat by your side and there comes a new perspective, a new understanding of the philosophy of life itself.

Edward E. Whiting [1875–?]

Think of her beautiful gliding form,
Her tread that would scarcely crush a worm,
And her soothing song by the winter fire,
Soft as the dying throb of a lyre.

William Wordsworth [1770–1850]

It is a difficult matter to gain the affection of a cat. He is a philosophical, methodical animal, tenacious of his own habits, fond of order and neatness, and disinclined to extravagant sentiment. He will be your friend, if he finds you worthy of friendship, but not your slave. Once it has given its love, what absolute confidence, what fidelity of affection! It will make itself the companion of your hours of work, of loneliness, of sadness. It will lie the whole evening on your knee, purring and happy in your society, and leaving the company of creatures of its own society to be with you.

Théophile Gautier [1811–72]

On the Death of a Cat
A Friend of Mine Aged Ten Years and a Half
Who shall tell the lady's grief
When her Cat was past relief?
Who shall number the hot tears
Shed o'er her, belov'd for years?

Who shall say the dark dismay
Which her dying caused that day?

Come, ye Muses, one and all,
Come obedient to my call;
Come and mourn with tuneful breath
Each one for a separate death....

And whoever passes by
The poor grave where Puss doth lie,
Softly, softly let him tread,
Nor disturb her narrow bed.

Christina Rossetti [1830–94]

My Cat Jeoffry

For I will consider my Cat Jeoffry.

For he is the servant of the Living God, duly and
daily serving him.

For at the first glance of the glory of God in the
East he worships in his way.

For is this done by wreathing his body seven
times round with elegant quickness.

For then he leaps up to catch the musk, which is
the blessing of God upon his prayer.

For he rolls upon prank to work it in.

For having done duty and received blessing he
begins to consider himself.

For this he performs in ten degrees.

For first he looks upon his fore-paws to see if
they are clean.

For secondly he kicks up behind to clear away
there.
For thirdly he works it upon stretch with the
fore-paws extended.
For fourthly he sharpens his paws by wood.
For fifthly he washes himself.
For sixthly he rolls upon wash.
For seventhly he fleas himself, that he may not
be interrupted upon the beat.
For eighthly he rubs himself against a post.
For ninthly he looks up for his instruction.
For tenthly he goes in quest of food.
For having consider'd God and himself he will
consider his neighbor.
For if he meets another cat he will kiss her in
kindness.
For when he takes his prey he plays with it to
give it a chance.
For one mouse in seven escapes by his dallying.
For when his day's work is done his business
more properly begins.
For he keeps the Lord's watch in the night
against the adversary.
For he counteracts the powers of darkness by his
electrical skin & glaring eyes.
For he counteracts the Devil, who is death, by
brisking about the life.
For in his morning orisons he loves the sun and
the sun loves him.

For he is of the tribe of Tiger.

For the Cherub Cat is a term of the Angel Tiger.

For he has the subtlety and hissing of a serpent,
which in goodness he suppresses.

For he will not do destruction, if he is well-fed,
neither will he spit without provocation.

For he purrs in thankfulness, when God tells him
he's a good Cat.

For he is an instrument for the children to learn
benevolence upon.

For every house is incompleat without him & a
blessing is lacking in the spirit.

Christopher Smart [1722–71]

Excerpts from a Cat's Diary

Day 752

My captors continue to taunt me with bizarre little dangling objects. They dine lavishly on fresh meat, while I am forced to eat dry cereal. The only thing that keeps me going is the hope of escape, and the mild satisfaction I get from occasionally ruining a piece of furniture. Tomorrow I may eat another houseplant.

Day 761

Today my attempt to kill my captors by weaving around their feet while they were walking almost succeeded; must try this at the top of the stairs. In an attempt to disgust and repulse these vile oppressors, I once again induced myself to vomit on their favorite chair; must try this on their bed.

Day 765
Decapitated a mouse and brought them the headless body, an attempt to make them aware of what I am capable of, and to try to strike fear into their hearts. They only cooed and condescended about what a good little cat I was...Hmmm. Not working according to plan.

Day 768
I am finally aware of how sadistic they are. For no good reason I was chosen for the water torture. This time, however, it included a burning foamy chemical called "shampoo." What sick minds could invent such a liquid? My only consolation is the piece of thumb still stuck between my teeth.

Day 771
There was some sort of gathering of their accomplices. I was placed in solitary throughout the event. However, I could hear the noise and smell the foul odor of the glass tubes they call "beer." More importantly, I overheard that my confinement was due to MY power of "allergies." Must learn what this is and how to use it to my advantage.

Day 774

I am convinced the other captives are flunkies and maybe snitches. The dog is routinely released and seems more than happy to return. He is obviously a half-wit. The bird on the other hand has got to be an informant, and speaks with them regularly. I am certain he reports my every move. Due to his current placement in the metal room his safety is assured. But I can wait, it is only a matter of time....   *author unknown*

For Dogs

Excerpts from a Dog's Diary
Day 180
  8:00 A.M.—
    OH BOY! DOG FOOD! MY FAVORITE!
  9:30 A.M.—
    OH BOY! A CAR RIDE! MY FAVORITE!
  9:40 A.M.—
    OH BOY! A WALK! MY FAVORITE!
  10:30 A.M.—
    OH BOY! A CAR RIDE! MY FAVORITE!
  11:30 A.M.—
    OH BOY! DOG FOOD! MY FAVORITE!
  Noon—
    OH BOY! THE KIDS! MY FAVORITE!
  1:00 P.M.—
    OH BOY! THE YARD! MY FAVORITE!

4:00 P.M.—

OH BOY! THE KIDS! MY FAVORITE!

5:00 P.M.—

OH BOY! DOG FOOD! MY FAVORITE!

5:30 P.M.—

OH BOY! MOM! MY FAVORITE!

Day 181

8:00 A.M.—

OH BOY! DOG FOOD! MY FAVORITE!

9:30 A.M.—

OH BOY! A CAR RIDE! MY FAVORITE!

9:40 A.M.—

OH BOY! A WALK! MY FAVORITE!

10:30 A.M.—

OH BOY! A CAR RIDE! MY FAVORITE!

11:30 A.M.—

OH BOY! DOG FOOD! MY FAVORITE!

Noon—

OH BOY! THE KIDS! MY FAVORITE!

1:00 P.M.—

OH BOY! THE YARD! MY FAVORITE!

4:00 P.M.—

OH BOY! THE KIDS! MY FAVORITE!

5:00 P.M.—

OH BOY! DOG FOOD! MY FAVORITE!

5:30 P.M.—

OH BOY! MOM! MY FAVORITE!

Day 182
>   8:00 A.M.—
>   OH BOY! DOG FOOD! MY FAVORITE!
>   9:30 A.M.—
>   OH BOY! A CAR RIDE! MY FAVORITE!
>   9:40 A.M.—
>   OH BOY! A WALK! MY FAVORITE
>   10:30 A.M.—
>   OH BOY! A CAR RIDE! MY FAVORITE!
>   11:30 A.M.—
>   OH BOY! DOG FOOD! MY FAVORITE!
>   Noon—
>   OH BOY! THE KIDS! MY FAVORITE!
>   1:00 P.M.—
>   OH BOY! THE YARD! MY FAVORITE!
>   1:30 P.M.—
>   ooooooo. bath. bummer.
>   4:00 P.M.—
>   OH BOY! THE KIDS! MY FAVORITE!
>   5:00 P.M.—
>   OH BOY! DOG FOOD! MY FAVORITE!
>   5:30 P.M.—
>   OH BOY! MOM! MY FAVORITE!

author unknown

Not the least hard thing to bear when they go from us, these quiet friends, is that they carry away with them so many years of our lives. Yet, if they find warmth therein, who would begrudge them those years that they have so guarded? And whatever they take, be sure they have deserved.

John Galsworthy [1867–1933]

Heaven's Doggy-Door
My best friend closed his eyes last night,
As his head was in my hand.
The doctors said he was in pain,
And it was hard for him to stand.

The thoughts that scurried through my head,
As I cradled him in my arms,
Were of his younger, puppy years,
And O, his many charms.

Today, there was no gentle nudge
With an intense "I love you" gaze,
Only a heart that's filled with tears
Remembering our joy-filled days.

But an angel just appeared to me,
And he said, "You should cry no more.
God also loves our canine friends:
He's installed a 'doggy-door'!"   *Mary Ellen Arthur*

The more I see of humankind, the more I love my dog.

Blaise Pascal [1623–62]

I, who had had my heart full for hours, took advantage of an early moment of solitude, to cry in it very bitterly. Suddenly a little hairy head thrust itself from behind my pillow into my face, rubbing its ears and nose against me in a responsive agitation, and drying the tears as they came.

Elizabeth Barrett Browning [1806–61]

The Dogs Who Have Shared Our Lives
The dogs who've shared our lives,
In subtle ways they let us know
their spirit still survives.
Old habits make us think
we hear a barking at the door.
Or step back when we drop
a tasty morsel on the floor.
Our feet still go around the place
the food dish used to be,
And sometimes, coming home at night,
we miss them terribly.
And although time may bring new friends
and a new food dish to fill,
That one place in our hearts
belongs to them...
And always will.

Linda Barnes

You know, of course, that by nature the disposition of noble dogs is to be as gentle as can be with their familiars and people they know and the opposite with those they don't know....And when it sees someone it knows, it greets him warmly, even if it never had a good experience with him....And so, how can it be anything other than

a lover of learning since it defines what's its own
and what's alien by knowledge and ignorance?

Socrates [470?–399 B.C.E.]

He is your friend, your partner, your defender,
your dog. You are his life, his love, his leader. He
will be yours, faithful and true, to the last beat of
his heart. You owe it to him to be worthy of such
devotion.   *author unknown*

If you pick up a starving dog and make him pros-
perous, he will not bite you. This is the principal
difference between a dog and a man.

Mark Twain [1835–1910]

Nobody can fully understand the meaning of love
unless he's owned a dog. A dog can show you more
honest affection with a flick of his tail than a man
can gather through a lifetime of handshakes.

Gene Hill [1928–97]

Histories are more full of the examples of the
fidelity of dogs than of friends.

Alexander Pope [1688–1744]

Dogs are our link to paradise. They don't know evil
or jealousy or discontent. To sit with a dog on a
hillside on a glorious afternoon is to be back in
Eden, where doing nothing was not boring—it was
peace.   *Milan Kundera*

There is no psychiatrist in the world like a puppy
licking your face.   *Ben Williams*

––––––––––––

No matter how little money and how few possessions you own, having a dog makes you rich.

Louis Sabin

––––––––––––

The Best Part about Owning a Dog...

...is the way he will come over to see me, for no reason, just to let me know I'm important to him.

...is the way she is always ready to lick the jelly off
my nose.

...is the way he looks into my eyes and finds con-
tentment in simply being near me.

...is the way she will run all over the yard, fetch a
soggy tennis ball and bring it back to me as if to
say, "Look, Mom, it's all I have, but it's yours."

...is the way he wakes me up in the morning by
pushing his cold, wet nose in my ear and snuff-
ing loudly.

...is the way she shreds toilet paper all over the
house, because it's fun, even though she knows
she shouldn't.

...is the way he's sure he can catch the ducks in the
lake today.

...is the way she comes over to me when she is sad.

...is the way he wedges himself near me when I am
sad and pushes all others away, to console me
with his love.

...is the way she pounces on crickets in the backyard.

...is the way he looks perplexed when they escape.

...is the way she is terrified of the evil pink Hula
Hoop.

...is the way he doesn't mind how much of that hor-
rid perfume I'm wearing just because it was a gift
from my relative who's visiting.

...is the way she doesn't care about bad hair days or
overdue bills.

...is the way he loves me, even when I'm impatient
with him and have no time this morning for a
game of tug-of-war.

...is the way her coat feels like liquid silk under my
fingers.

...is the way he finds wisdom beyond words.

author unknown

If a dog will not come to you after having looked
you in the face, you should go home and examine
your conscience.   *Woodrow Wilson [1856–1924]*

To err is human; to forgive, canine.   *author unknown*

Message from a Departed Friend
I explained to Saint Peter,
    I'd rather stay here
Outside the pearly gate.

I won't be a nuisance,
  I won't even bark,
I'll be very patient and wait.

I'll be here, chewing on a celestial bone,
  No matter how long you may be.

I'd miss you so much if I went in alone,
  It wouldn't be heaven to me.   *author unknown*

_____

Old Blue died and he died so hard,
Shook the ground in my backyard.
Dug his grave with a silver spade,
Lowered him down with links of chain.
With every link I did call his name:
"Here, Blue, you good dog you.
Here, Blue, I'm a coming too!"

                    American folksong

_____

A dog is the only thing on this earth that loves you
more than he loves himself.

          Josh Billings [Henry Wheeler Shaw] [1818–85]

_____

The time comes to every dog when it ceases to
care for people merely for biscuits or bones, or
even for caresses and walks out-of-doors. When a
dog really loves, it prefers the person who gives it
nothing, and perhaps is too ill ever to take it out
for exercise....   *Frances P. Cobbe [1822–1904]*

_____

The dog was created especially for children. He is
the god of frolic.   *Henry Ward Beecher [1813–87]*

The dog hesitated for a moment, but presently
made some little advances with his tail. The child
put out his hand and called him. In an apologetic
manner the dog came close, and the two had an
interchange of friendly pattings and waggles.

Stephen Crane [1871–1900]

My little old dog;
A heart-beat at my feet.   *Edith Wharton [1862–1937]*

She Lets Us Love Her
Just to be loving.
Just to be loved.
How few of us know that is enough!

My dog is very much a dog;
she does nothing
except what a dog should do,
which is largely nothing.
She is not even an especially affectionate dog—
she does not leap on us
when we come home
or cover us with wet kisses;
but in a quiet way,
like some human beings,
she shows us that she loves us.

She is a beautiful dog,
though not even that in everyone's eyes.
But she does none of the things
we human beings have come to feel
are necessary:
she does not possess a fortune;
she does no useful work;
she has no fame
or important position in the community;
she shows no exceptional talent.
She does no great feats
so that we can brag about her to the neighbors.
She does not even guard the house
or do clever tricks for company.

She does only one thing—
she lets us love her.
No more than this,
but this is enough.

She needs no other reason for being
except
to let us love her.

Love justifies all the expense and care
we lavish on her
and compensates us for the nuisance
she sometimes is—
like every living thing.

Just to be loved.
Just to be loving.
This is reason enough for being.
Have you ever thought of that?

You there pursuing so intently
all those grand schemes
and lofty ambitions
you feel you have to pursue
in order to be of value—
you there striving so hard—
for what?
My dog lets me love her—
no more than this—
and that is reason enough—
and more—
for her to be.

How glad I am
that we found her
and have her living with us.
My wife and I are willing to be
her maid and cook and nurse and companion and
    provider.
There she lies
stretched out indolently on the floor,
and she lets me pet her,
if I will take the trouble to bend down.
I look at her
and I know something

more about life
than I knew without her.
I know what is necessary and important—
and what is not.   *James Dillet Freeman [1912–2003]*

_____

The great pleasure of a dog is that you may make
a fool of yourself with him and not only will he not
scold you, he will make a fool of himself too.

Samuel Butler [1835–1902]

_____

The most affectionate creature in the world is a
wet dog.   *Ambrose Bierce [1842–1914]*

_____

Dogs are much superior to human beings as companions. They do not quarrel or argue with you.
They never talk about themselves but listen to you
while you talk about yourself, and keep up an
appearance of being interested in the conversa-
tion. They never make stupid remarks.

They never say unkind things. They never tell us
our faults, "merely for our own good." They do not
at inconvenient moments mildly remind us of our
past follies and mistakes. They never inform us, as
our inamoratas sometimes do, that we are not
nearly so nice as we used to be. We are always the
same to them. He is very imprudent, a dog is. He
never makes it his business to inquire whether you
are in the right or in the wrong, never bothers as to
whether you are going up or down upon life's lad-
der, never asks whether you are rich or poor, silly or

wise, sinner or saint. You are his pal. That is enough for him, and come luck, or misfortune, good repute or bad, honor or shame, he is going to stick to you, to comfort you, guard you, give his life for you, if need be.... *Jerome K. Jerome [1859–1927]*

———————

To My Setter, Scout
You are a tried and loyal friend;
    The end
  Of life will find you leal, unweary
Of tested bonds that naught can rend,
  And e'en though years be sad and dreary
Our plighted friendship will extend.

A truer friend man never had;
    'Tis sad
  That 'mongst all earthly friends the fewest
Unfaithful ones should be clad
  In canine lowliness; yet truest
They, be their treatment good or bad.

Within your eyes methinks I find
    A kind
  And thoughtful look of speechless feeling
That mem'ry's loosened cords unbind,
  And let the dreamy past come stealing
Through your dumb, reflective mind.

Scout, my trusty friend, can it be
　　You see
　　Again, in retrospective dreaming,
The run, the woodland and the lea,
　　With past autumnal streaming
O'er every frost-dyed field and tree?

Or do you see now once again
　　The glen
　　And fern, the highland and the thistle,
And do you still remember when
　　We heard the bright-eyed woodcock whistle
Down by the rippling shrub-edged fen?

I see you turn a listening ear
　　To hear
　　The quail upon the flower-pied heather;
But, doggie, wait till uplands sere
　　And then the autumn's waning weather
Will bring the sport we hold so dear.

Then we will hunt the loamy swale
　　And trail
　　The snipe, their cunning wiles o'ercoming,
And oft will flush the bevied quail,
　　And hear the partridge slowly drumming
Dull echoes in the leaf-strewn dale.

When wooded hills with crimson light
　　Are bright
　　We'll stroll where trees and vines are growing,

And see birds warp their southern flight
    At sundown, when the Day King's throwing
Sly kisses to the Queen of Night.

When shadows fall in life's fair dell,
    And knell
    Of death comes with the autumn's ev'n
To separate us, who can tell
    But that, within the realm of heaven,
We both together there will dwell?

                         Frank H. Selden [1866–?]

The Curate Thinks You Have No Soul
The curate thinks you have no soul;
    I know that he has none. But you,
Dear friend, whose solemn self-control,
    In our foursquare familiar pew,
Was pattern to my youth—whose bark
    Called me in summer dawns to rove—
Have you gone down into the dark
    Where none is welcome—none may love?
I will not think those good brown eyes
    Have spent their life of truth so soon;
But in some canine paradise
    Your wraith, I know, rebukes the moon,
And quarters every plain and hill,
    Seeking his master…As for me,
This prayer at least the gods fulfill:
    That when I pass the flood and see

Old Charon by the Stygian coast
   Take toll of all the shades who land,
Your little, faithful, barking ghost
   May leap to lick my phantom hand.

St. John Welles Lucas [1829–1934]

To John, My Collie
So you have left me. Here's the end,
My loyal comrade, fellow, friend,
You've had your day, as all dogs must,
Nor all your love and faith and trust
Could keep you with me—fellow, friend,
You've run your race and here's the end.

No not the end! For how shall I
Lay claim to immortality,
If naught your faith and love and trust
Availed to save your soul from dust?
Out of your brown eyes looked at me
A very soul, if souls there be,
And when at Peter's gate I knock
And Peter's keys hear in the lock,
And hear not any answering bark,
I'll face again into the dark,
From star to star, through God's wide space,
Until I find your dwelling place.

And when I find you where you dwell,
Perchance in fields of asphodel,
…no gates there are

Can hold you back, nor any bar,
Nor angel with the flaming sword,
When once you hear your master's word....

And so once more our way we'll wend,
To outer darkness, friend and friend,
Nor lack for any light, we two,
So you have me and I have you...

Walter Thomson Peirce [1875–?]

Jack
Dog Jack has gone on the silent trail,
Wherever that may be;
But well I know, when I whistle the call,
He will joyfully answer me.
That call will be when I, myself,
Have passed through the Gates of God;
He will come with a rush, and his soft brown eyes
Will glisten with love as of old.
Oh, Warder of Gates, in the far away land,
This little black dog should you see,
Throw wide your doors that this faithful friend
May enter, and wait for me. *H. P. W.*

To a Dog
On every side I see your trace;
Your water-trough's scarce dry;
Your empty collar in its place
Provokes the heavy sigh.

And you were here two days ago.
There's little changed, I see.
The sun is just as bright, but oh!
The difference to me!...   *author unknown*

———————————

Where to Bury a Dog
Beneath a cherry tree, or an apple, or any flowering shrub of the garden, is an excellent place to bury a good dog. Beneath such trees, such shrubs, he slept in the drowsy summer, or gnawed at a flavorous bone, or lifted head to challenge some strange intruder. These are good places, in life or in death. Yet it is a small matter, and it touches sentiment more than anything else. For if the dog be well remembered, if sometimes he leaps through your dreams actual as in life, eyes kindling, questing, asking, laughing, begging, it matters not at all where that dog sleeps at long and at last. On a hill where the wind is unrebuked, and the trees are roaring, or beside a stream he knew in puppyhood, or somewhere in the flatness of a pasture land.... It is all one to the dog, and all one to you, and nothing is gained, and nothing lost—if memory lives. But there is one best place to bury a dog. One place that is best of all.

If you bury him in this spot, the secret of which you must already have, he will come to you when you call—come to you over the grim, dim frontiers of death, and down the well-remembered path, and to your side again. And though you call a dozen living dogs to heel they should not growl at him, nor resent his coming, for he is yours and he belongs there. People may scoff at you, who see no lightest blade of grass bent by his footfall, who hear no whimper pitched too fine for mere audition, people who may never really have had a dog. Smile at them then, for you shall know something that is hidden from them, and which is well worth the knowing. The one best place to bury a good dog is in the heart of his master.

Ben Hur Lampman [1886–1954]

The Last Will and Testament of Silverdene Emblem O'Neill

One last word of farewell, Dear Master and Mistress. Whenever you visit my grave, say to yourselves with regret but also with happiness in your hearts at the remembrance of my long happy life with you: "Here lies one who loved us and whom we loved." No matter how deep my sleep I shall hear you, and not all the power of death can keep my spirit from wagging a grateful tail.

Eugene O'Neill [1888–1953]

Of course what he most intensely dreams of is being taken out on walks, and the more you are able to indulge him the more will he adore you and

the more all the latent beauty of his nature will
come out.   *Henry James [1843–1916]*

A score of times I have told him that he had much
better not come; I have announced fiercely that he
is not to come. He then lets go of his legs...and,
laying his head between his front paws, stares at
me through the red haws that make his eyes so
mournful. He will do this for an hour without
blinking, for he knows that in time it will unman
me. My dog knows very little, but what little he
does know he knows extraordinarily well. One can
get out of my chambers by a back way, and I sometimes steal softly—but I can't help looking back,
and there he is, and there are those haws asking
sorrowfully, "Is this worthy of you?" "Curse you," I
say, "get your hat," or words to that effect....

                    J. M. Barrie [1860–1937]

Dog, *n.* A kind of additional or subsidiary Deity
designed to catch the overflow and surplus of the
world's worship. This Divine Being in some of his
smaller and silkier incarnations, takes, in the
affection of Woman, the place to which there is no
human male aspirant. The Dog is a survival—an
anachronism. He toils not, neither does he spin,
yet Solomon in all his glory never lay upon a door-
mat all day long, sun-soaked and fly-fed and fat,
while his master worked for the means wherewith

to purchase an idle wag of the Solomonic tail, seasoned with a look of tolerant recognition.

Ambrose Bierce [1842–1914]

I must tell you a feat of my dog Beau. Walking by the river side, I observed some water-lilies floating at a little distance from the bank. They are a large white flower, with an orange-colored eye, very beautiful. I had a desire to gather one, and, having your long cane in my hand, by the help of it endeavored to bring one of them within my reach. But the attempt proved vain, and I walked forward.

Beau had all the while observed me attentively. Returning soon after toward the same place, I observed him plunge into the river, while I was about forty yards distance from him, and, when I had nearly reached the spot, he swam to land with a lily in his mouth, which he came and laid at my foot.   *William Cowper [1731–1800]*

Things We Can Learn from a Dog

1. Never pass up the opportunity to go for a joy ride.
2. Allow the experience of fresh air and the wind in your face to be pure ecstasy.
3. When loved ones come home, always run to greet them.
4. When it's in your best interest, always practice obedience.

5. Let others know when they've invaded your territory.
6. Take naps, and always stretch before rising.
7. Run, romp, and play daily.
8. Eat with gusto and enthusiasm.
9. Be loyal.
10. Never pretend to be something you're not.
11. If what you want lies buried, dig until you find it.
12. When someone is having a bad day, be silent, sit close by, and nuzzle them gently.
13. Delight in the simple joy of a long walk.
14. Thrive on attention, and let people touch you.
15. Avoid biting when a simple growl will do.
16. On hot days, drink lots of water and lie under a shady tree.
17. When you are happy, dance around and wag your entire body.
18. No matter how often you are criticized, don't buy into the guilt thing and pout. Run right back and make friends.   *author unknown*

Epitaph for a Small Dog
Here rests a little dog
Whose feet ran never faster
Than when they took the path
Leading to his master.   *LeBaron Cooke*

Bishop Doane on His Dog
I am quite sure he thinks that I am God—

Since he is God on whom each one depends
For life, and all things that His bounty sends—
My dear old dog, most constant of all friends;
Not quick to mind, but quicker far than I
To Him whom God I know and own; his eye,
Deep brown and liquid, watches for my nod;
He is more patient underneath the rod
Than I, when God His wise correction sends.

He looks love at me, deep as words e'er spake;
And from me never crumb nor sup will take
But he wags thanks with his most vocal tail;
And when some crashing noise wakes all his fear,
He is content and quiet, if I am near,
Secure that my protection will prevail.
So, faithful, mindful, thankful, trustful, he
Tells me what I unto my God should be.

George Washington Doane [1799–1859]

Epitaph to a Dog

Near this spot
Are deposited the Remains
of one
Who possessed Beauty
Without Vanity,
Strength without Insolence,
Courage without Ferocity,
And all the Virtues of Man
Without his Vice.

This Praise, which would be unmeaning flattery
If inscribed over Human Ashes,
Is but a just tribute to the Memory of
"Boatswain," a Dog
Who was born at Newfoundland,
May 1, 1803,
And died at Newstead Abbey
Nov. 18, 1808.

When some proud son of man returns to earth,
Unknown to glory, but upheld by birth,
The sculptor's art exhausts the pomp of woe,
And storied urns record who rests below.
When all is done, upon the tomb is seen,
Not what he was, but what he should have been.
But the poor dog, in life the firmest friend,
The first to welcome, foremost to defend,
Whose honest heart is still his master's own,
Who labors, fights, lives, breathes for him alone,
Unhonored falls, unnoticed all his worth,
Denied in heaven the soul he held on earth—
While man, vain insect! hopes to be forgiven,
And claims himself a sole exclusive heaven.

Oh man! thou feeble tenant of an hour,
Debased by slavery, or corrupt by power—
Who knows thee well must quit thee with disgust,
Degraded mass of animated dust!
Thy love is lust, thy friendship all a cheat,
Thy smiles hypocrisy, thy words deceit!

By nature vile, ennobled but by name,
Each kindred brute might bid thee blush for shame.

Ye, who perchance behold this simple urn,
Pass on—it honors none you wish to mourn.
To mark a friend's remains these stones arise;
I never knew but one—and here he lies.

Lord Byron [1788–1824]

———————

I have sometimes thought of the final cause of
dogs having such short lives and I am quite satisfied it is in compassion to the human race; for if
we suffer so much in loving a dog after an
acquaintance of ten or twelve years, what would it
be if they were to live double that time?

Sir Walter Scott [1771–1832]

———————

To a Dog
So, back again?
    —And is your errand done,
Unfailing one?
How quick the gray world, at your morning look,
Turns wonder book!
Come in—O guard and guest;
Come, O you breathless, from a lifelong quest!
Search my heart; and if a comfort be,
Ah, comfort me.
You eloquent one, you best
Of all diviners, so to trace
The weather gleams upon a face;

With wordless, querying paw,
Adventuring the law!
You shaggy Loveliness,
What call was it?—What dream beyond a guess,
Lured you, gray ages back,
From that lone bivouac
Of the wild pack?—
Was it your need or ours? The calling trail
Of Faith that should not fail?
Of hope dim understood?—
That you should follow our poor humanhood,
Only because you would!
To search and circle—follow and outstrip,
Men and their fellowship;
And keep your heart no less,
Your to-and-fro of hope and wistfulness,
Through all world-weathers and against all odds!

Can you forgive us, now?—
Your fallen gods?   *Josephine Preston Peabody* [1874–1922]

I Think I Know No Finer Things Than Dogs
Though prejudice perhaps my mind befogs,
I think I know no finer things than dogs:
The young ones, they of gay and bounding heart,
Who lure us in their games to take a part,
Who with mock tragedy their antics cloak
And, from their wild eyes' tail, admit the joke;
The old ones, with their wistful, fading eyes,
They who desire no further paradise

Than the warm comfort of our smile and hand,
Who tune their moods to ours and understand
Each word and gesture; they who lie and wait
To welcome us—with no rebuke if late.
Sublime the love they bear; but ask to live
Close to our feet, unrecompensed to give;
Beside which many men seem very logs—
I think I know no finer things than dogs.

Hally Carrington Brent

Bum

He's a little dog, with a stubby tail, and a
    moth-eaten coat of tan,
  And his legs are short, of the wabbly sort;
I doubt if they ever ran;
And he howls at night, while in broad daylight
    he sleeps like a bloomin' log,
And he likes the food of the gutter breed; he's a
    most irregular dog.

I call him Bum, and in total sum he's all that his
    name implies,
For he's just a tramp with a highway stamp that
    culture cannot disguise;
And his friends, I've found, in the streets abound,
    be they urchins or dogs or men;
  Yet he sticks to me with a fiendish glee. It is
    truly beyond my ken.

I talk to him when I'm lonesome-like, and I'm
    sure that he understands
When he looks at me so attentively and gently
    licks my hands;
Then he rubs his nose on my tailored clothes, but
    I never say nought thereat,
For the good Lord knows I can buy more clothes,
    but never a friend like that!

W. Dayton Wedgefarth

———————

So great is my need of a comrade, an untalking companion, on my walks, or boating, or about the farm; and, next to one's bosom friend, what companion like a dog? Your thought is his thought, your wish is his wish, and where you desire to go, that place of all others is preferable to him. It was bliss enough for Rab to be with me, and it was a never-failing source of pleasure for me to be with Rab....

My dog is interested in everything I do. Then he represents the spirit of holiday, of fun, of adventure. The world is full of wonders to him, and in a journey of a mile he has many adventures. Every journey is an excursion, a sally into an unknown land, teeming with curiosities. A dog lives only ten or fifteen years, but think how much he crowds into that space, how much energy and vitality he lives up!   *John Burroughs [1837–1921]*

———————

My Dog
I have no dog, but it must be
Somewhere there's one belongs to me—
A little chap with wagging tail,
And dark brown eyes that never quail,
But look you through, and through, and through,
With love unspeakable and true.

Somewhere it must be, I opine,
There is a little dog of mine
With cold black nose that sniffs around
In search of what things may be found
In pocket or some nook hard by
Where I have hid them from his eye.

Somewhere my doggie pulls and tugs
The fringes of rebellious rugs,
Or with the mischief of the pup
Chews all my shoes and slippers up,
And when he's done it to the core,
With eyes all eager, pleads for more.

Somewhere upon his hinder legs
My little doggie sits and begs,
And in a wistful minor tone
Pleads for the pleasures of the bone—
I pray it be his owner's whim
To yield, and grant the same to him.

Somewhere a little dog doth wait;
It may be by some garden gate.

With eyes alert and tail attent—
You know the kind of tail that's meant—
With stores of yelps of glad delight
To bid me welcome home at night.

Somewhere a little dog is seen,
His nose two shaggy paws between,
Flat on his stomach, one eye shut
Held fast in dreamy slumber, but
The other open, ready for
His master coming through the door.

John Kendrick Bangs [1862–1922]

The Malemute
You can't tell me God would have Heaven
    So a man couldn't mix with his friends—
That we are doomed to meet disappointment
    When we come to the place the trail ends.

That would be a low-grade sort of Heaven,
    And I'd never regret a damned sin
If I rush up to the gates white and pearly,
    And they don't let my malemute in.

For I know it would never be homelike
    No matter how golden the strand,
If I lose out that pal-loving feeling
    Of a malemute's nose on my hand.

Pat O'Cotter

Gentlemen of the jury. The best friend a man has in this world may turn against him and become his enemy. His son and daughter that he has reared with loving care may become ungrateful. Those who are nearest and dearest to us, those whom we trust with our happiness and our good name, may become traitors to their faith. The money that a man has he may lose. It flies away from him when he may need it most. Man's reputation may be sacrificed in a moment of ill-considered action. The people who are prone to fall on their knees and do us honor when success is with us may be the first to throw the stone of malice when failure settles its cloud upon our heads. The one absolutely unselfish friend a man may have in this selfish world, the one that never deserts him, the one that never proves ungrateful or treacherous, is the dog.

Gentlemen of the jury, a man's dog stands by him in prosperity and poverty, in health and in sickness. He will sleep on the cold ground when the wintry winds blow and the snow drives fiercely, if only he may be near his master's side. He will kiss the hand that has no food to offer, he will lick the wounds and sores that come in encounter with the roughness of the world. He guards the sleep of his pauper master as if he were a prince.

When all other friends desert, he remains. When riches take wings and reputation falls to pieces, he is as constant in his love as the sun in its journey through the heavens. If fortune drives the master forth an outcast into the world, friendless and homeless, the faithful dog asks no higher privilege than that of accompanying him, to guard him against danger, to fight against his enemies, and when the last scene of all comes, and death takes his master in its embrace and his body is laid in the cold ground, no matter if all other friends pursue their way, there by his graveside will the noble dog be found, his head between his paws and his eyes sad, but open, in alert watchfulness and true, even unto death.

Senator George Graham Vest [1830–1904]

For Birds

Hope is the thing with feathers
That perches in the soul.
And sings the tune without the words
And never stops at all,

And sweetest in the gale is heard;
And sore must be the storm
That could abash the little bird
That kept so many warm.

I've heard it in the chillest land,
And on the strangest sea,

Yet, never, in extremity,
It asked a crumb of me.   *Emily Dickinson [1830–86]*

I walked out alone in the evening and heard the birds singing in the full chorus of song, which can only be heard at that time of the year at dawn or at sunset....A lark rose suddenly from the ground beside the tree by which I was standing and poured out its song above my head and then sank still singing to rest. Everything then grew still as the sunset faded and the veil of dusk began to cover the earth. I remember now the feeling of awe which came over me. I felt inclined to kneel to the ground, as though I had been standing in the presence of an angel; and I hardly dared to look on the face of the sky, because it seemed as though it was but a veil before the face of God.

Bede Griffiths [1906–93]

This sparrow died today, O Lord,
Your feathered creature small.
We lay him in the friendly earth
And ask Your blessing on us all.   *Esther Wilkin*

It happened in a park where a flock of wild geese had settled to rest on a pond. One of the flock had been captured by a gardener, who had clipped its wings before releasing it. When the geese started to resume their flight, this one tried frantically, but vainly, to lift itself into the air. The others, observing his struggles, flew about in obvious efforts to encourage him; but it was no use. Thereupon the entire flock settled back on the pond and waited, even though the urge to go on was strong within them. For several days they waited until the damaged feathers had grown sufficiently to permit the goose to fly. Meanwhile the unethical gardener, having been converted by the ethical geese, gladly watched them as they finally rose together, and resumed their long flight.

Albert Schweitzer [1875–1965]

[A] friend in Hannover, who owned a small café... would daily throw out crumbs for the sparrows in the neighborhood. He noticed that one sparrow was injured, so that it had difficulty getting about. But he was interested to discover that the other sparrows, apparently by mutual agreement, would leave the crumbs which lay nearest their crippled comrade, so that he could get his share, undisturbed.

Albert Schweitzer [1875–1965]

Did You Ever Hear an English Sparrow Sing?
    What? An English sparrow sing?
    Insignificant brown thing,
So common and so bold, 'twould surely bring
    Tears of laughter to the eyes
    Of the superficial wise
To suggest that that small immigrant could sing.

'Twas the bleakest wintry day,
Earth, sky, water, all were gray,
Of the universe old Boreas seemed king,
As he swept across the lake,
But his empire was at stake,
When that little English sparrow dared to sing.

Not a friend on earth had I,
No horizon to my sky,
No faith that there could be another spring.
Cold the world as that gray wall
Of the Auditorium tall
Where I heard that little English sparrow sing.

On the shelving of one stone
He was cuddling all alone;
Oh, the little feet knew bravely how to cling!
As from out the tuneful throat
Came the sweetest, springlike note,
And I truly heard an English sparrow sing.

You may talk for all your days
In the thrush and bluebirds' praise
And all your other harbingers of spring,
But I've never heard a song
Whose echoes I'd prolong
Like that I heard that English sparrow sing.

Oh, my heart's a phonograph
That will register each laugh
And all happy sounds that from the joy-bells ring,

So if cloudy days should come,
In my hours of darkest gloom
I'm sure I'll hear that English sparrow sing.

Bertha Johnston [1864–?]

Three Things to Remember
A Robin Redbreast in a cage
Puts all Heaven in a rage.

A skylark wounded on the wing
Doth make a cherub cease to sing.

He who shall hurt the little wren
Shall never be beloved by men.

William Blake [1757–1827]

The very idea of a bird is a symbol and a suggestion
to the poet. A bird seems to be at the top of the scale,
so vehement and intense his life…. The beautiful
vagabonds, endowed with every grace, masters of all
climes, and knowing no bounds—how many human
aspirations are realised in their free, holiday-lives—
and how many suggestions to the poet in their flight
and song! *John Burroughs [1837–1921]*

The Canary
Mary had a little bird,
    With feathers bright and yellow,
Slender legs—upon my word,
    He was a pretty fellow!

Sweetest notes he always sung,
 Which much delighted Mary;
Often when his cage was hung,
 She sat to hear Canary.

Crumb of bread and dainty seeds
 She carried to him daily:
Seeking for the early weeds,
 She deck'd his palace gaily.

This, my little readers, learn,
 And ever practice duly;
Songs and smiles of love return
 To friends who love you truly.

Elizabeth Turner

I once had a sparrow alight upon my shoulder for a
moment, while I was hoeing in a village garden, and
I felt that I was more distinguished by that circum-
stance than I should have been by any epaulet I
could have worn.   *Henry David Thoreau [1817–62]*

Ringneck Parrots
The ringneck parrots, in scattered flocks,
The ringneck parrots are screaming in their
 upward flight.

The ringneck parrots are a cloud of wings;
The shell parrots are a cloud of wings.

Let the shell parrots come down to rest,
Let them come down to rest on the ground!

Let the caps fly off the scented blossoms!
Let the blooms descend to the ground in a shower!

The clustering bloodwood blooms are falling down,
The clustering bloodwood blossoms, nipped by
   birds.

The clustering bloodwood blooms are falling down,
The clustering bloodwood blossoms, one by one.

Aranda, Australia; translated by T. G. H. Strehlow

Parrots
parrots
with vermilion bands and beak
green-iris camouflaging
are acrobats
swinging on trapezes of green gum leaves
tips

they carry their very own safety net
their green-yellow tail feathers
which spray out like palm fronds
parachuting   *Neil Paech*

Ver-Vert
   The public soon began to ferret
The hidden nest of so much merit,
And, spite of all the nuns' endeavours,
The fame of Ver-Vert filled all Nevers;
Nay, from Moulines folks came to stare at
The wondrous talent of this parrot;

And to fresh visitors, *ad libitum*,
Sister Sophie had to exhibit him.
Dressed in her tidiest robes, the virgin,
Forth from the convent cells emerging,
Brings the bright bird, and for his plumage
First challenges unstinted homage;
Then to his eloquence adverts,—
"What preacher's can surpass Ver-Vert's?
Truly, in oratory, few men
Equal this learned catechumen,
Fraught with the convent's choicest lessons,
And stuffed with piety's quintessence;
A bird most quick of apprehension,
With gifts and graces hard to mention;
Say, in what pulpit can you meet
A Chrysostom half so discreet,
Who'd follow, in his ghostly mission,
So close the fathers and tradition?"
Silent, meantime, the feathered hermit
Waits for the sister's gracious permit,
When, at a signal from his Mentor,
Quick on a course of speech he'll enter:
Not that he cares for human glory,
Bent but to save his auditory;
Hence he pours forth with so much unction,
That all his hearers feel compunction.

   Thus for a time did Ver-Vert dwell
Safe in his holy citadel;

Scholared like any well-bred abbé
And loved by many a cloistered Hebe;
You'd swear that he had crossed the same bridge
As any youth brought up in Cambridge.
Other monks starve themselves; but his skin
Was sleek, like that of a Franciscan,
And far more clean; for this grave Solon
Bathed every day in *eau de Cologne.*
Thus he indulged each guiltless gambol,
Blessed had he ne'er been doomed to ramble!

Jean Baptiste Louis Gresset [1709–77]

I Stood Tiptoe
Linger awhile upon some bending planks
That lean against a streamlet's rushy banks,
And watch intently Nature's gentle doings:
They will be found softer than ring-dove's cooings....

Sometimes goldfinches one by one will drop
From low hung branches; little space they stop;
But sip, and twitter, and their feathers sleek;
Then off at once, as in a wanton freak:
Or perhaps, to show their black, and golden wings,
Pausing upon their yellow flutterings.

John Keats [1795–1821]

Birds of Paradise
Golden-winged, silver-winged,
   Winged with flashing flame,
Such a flight of birds I saw,

Birds without a name:
Singing songs in their own tongue—
    Song of songs—they came.

One to another calling,
    Each answering each,
One to another calling
    In their proper speech:
High above my head they wheeled,
    Far out of reach.

On wings of flame they went and came
    With a cadenced clang:
    Their silver wings tinkled,
    Their golden wings rang;
The wind it whistled through their wings
    Where in heaven they sang.

They flashed and they darted
    Awhile before mine eyes,
Mounting, mounting, mounting still,
    In haste to scale the skies,
Birds without a nest on earth,
    Birds of Paradise.

Where the moon riseth not
    Nor sun seeks the west,
There to sing their glory
    Which they sing at rest,
There to sing their love-song
    When they sing their best:—

Not in any garden
That mortal foot hath trod,
Not in any flowering tree
That springs from earthly sod,
But in the garden where they dwell,
The Paradise of God.

Christina Rossetti [1830–94]

How Francis Preached to the Birds

...the most blessed father Francis was making a trip through the Spoleto valley. He came to a certain place near Bevagna where a very great number of birds of various kinds had congregated, namely, doves, crows, and some others popularly called daws. When the most blessed servant of God, Francis, saw them,...he left his companions in the road and ran eagerly toward the birds. When he was close enough to them, seeing that they were waiting expectantly for him, he greeted them in his usual way. But, not a little surprised that the birds did not rise in flight, as they usually do, he was filled with great joy and humbly begged them to listen to the word of God. Among the many things he spoke to them were these words that he added: "My brothers, birds, you should praise your Creator very much and always love him; he gave you feathers to clothe you, wings so that you can fly, and whatever else was necessary for you. God made you noble among his creatures, and he gave you a home in the purity of the air; though you neither sow nor reap, he nevertheless protects and governs you without any solicitude on your part." At these words...the birds, rejoicing in a wonderful way according to their nature, began to stretch their necks, extend their wings, open their mouths and gaze at him. And Francis... blessed them, and then, after he made the sign of the cross over them, he gave them permission to fly away to some other place.... And so it happened that, from that day on, he solicitously admonished all birds, all animals and reptiles, and even creatures that have no feeling, to praise and love their Creator....   *Thomas of Celano [c. 1200–c. 1255]*

For Fish

I was 8 years old when my goldfish died. I went to feed him. He was floating on top of the water. I ran for some salt because I had been told that salt revives goldfish. It didn't help, and I knew I had lost a friend. I also faced death for the first time. I knew what I wanted to do. Later that morning, I took him to the backyard and buried him, using a stick from a popsicle to mark the spot. Almost fifty years later, I still find satisfaction knowing that somewhere at my childhood home my goldfish is part of the earth—and remembered.   *Malcolm D. Kriger*

Fish
Quelle joie de vivre
Dans l'eau!
Slowly to gape through the waters,
Alone with the element;
To sink, and rise, and go to sleep with the waters;
To speak of endless inaudible wavelets into the
wave;
To breathe from the flood at the gills,
Fish-blood slowly running next to the flood,
extracting fish-fire;
To have the element under one, like a lover;
And to spring away with a curvetting click in the
air,
Provocative.
Dropping back with a slap on the face of the
flood.
And merging oneself!

To be a fish!
So utterly without misgiving
To be a fish
In the waters.   *D. H. Lawrence [1885–1930]*

[Francis] was moved by the same tender affection toward fish, too, when they were caught, and he had the chance, he threw them back into the water, commanding them to be careful lest they be caught again. Once when he was sitting in a boat near a port in the lake of Rieti, a certain fisherman,

who had caught a big fish...offered it kindly to
him. He accepted it joyfully and kindly and began
to call it *brother*; then placing it in the water outside the boat, he began devoutly to bless the name
of the Lord. And while he continued in prayer for
some time, the fish played in the water beside the
boat and did not go away from the place where it
had been put until his prayer was finished and the
holy man of God gave it permission to leave.

Thomas of Celano [c.1200–c. 1255]

For Rabbits

Scooter was a very small bundle of gray fur when
she was found by my daughter inside a box in the
parking lot of a shopping mall. The family could
not resist a bunny who was so cute and cuddly, and
a special place was created for her in my daughter's bedroom. Every morning as my daughter
dressed for school, Scooter would romp on her bed
to lift her spirits. The rest of the day she spent running around the house, taking the stairs at a
bound and playing with anyone who happened to
have the time and inclination.... When no one was
available for play, she would lie in the living room,
directly in front of the TV....

With each new day, Scooter became more like a
member of the family. She had her meals along
with everyone else and even went along on family

vacations and trips to the store…. She also became a kind of good luck mascot at my son's baseball games.

The years passed and my daughter became engaged. Although at first her fiancé insisted that Scooter could not live with them when they got married, that is exactly what happened….

Some people thought that my daughter and her husband were being silly to dote so on a rabbit, but they didn't know of the joy that Scooter gave them….   G. L.

Thumper and I became very close…. I'd sit on the back step and drink a cup of coffee and Thumper would let me stroke his long transparent ears. He would leap three feet in the air and kick wildly about or twist and run madly about—just for the fun of it. He was so comical to watch, he always made me smile. He enjoyed sleeping on my bed, usually in the company of one of the cats. During my naps, he'd think nothing of hopping up beside me and stretching out at my side….

Thumper brought joy into our lives with all of his funny ways. When Red Dog died, he was there to ease the hurt. Eleven days after Red Dog's death…my comical fat friend…died….

What can I say to you, but that I still feel the loss…. But at least, I guess, one thing that makes me happy is that I had…the privilege of having a

white and gray rabbit who could always make me
smile. K. F.

My Pet Hare

Yes—thou mayst eat thy bread, and lick the hand
That feeds thee; thou mayst frolic on the floor
At evening, and at night retire secure
To thy straw couch, and slumber unalarm'd;
For I have gain'd thy confidence, have pledged
All that is human in me, to protect
Thine unsuspecting gratitude and love.
If I survive thee, I will dig thy grave;
And, when I place thee in it, sighing say,
I knew at least one hare that had a friend.

William Cowper [1731–1800]

Once when [Francis] was staying at the town of
Greccio, a little rabbit that had been caught in a
trap was brought alive to him by a certain brother.
When the most blessed man saw it, he was moved
to pity and said: "Brother rabbit, come to me. Why
did you allow yourself to be deceived like this?" And
as soon as the rabbit had been let go by the brother
who held it, it fled to the saint, and, without being
forced by anyone, it lay quiet in his bosom as the
safest place possible. After he had rested there a
little while, the holy father, caressing it with moth-
erly affection, released it so it could return free to
the woods. But when it had been placed upon the

ground several times and had returned each time to the saint's bosom, he finally commanded it to be carried by the brothers to the nearby woods. Something similar happened with a certain rabbit, by nature a very wild creature, when he was on an island in the lake of Perugia.

Thomas of Celano [c. 1200–c. 1255]

For Ferrets, Mice, and Guinea Pigs

Natalie was a gold-and-white guinea pig, with full lips and an overstated stomach. She shared her life with us, accepted our love and care, nibbled daintily on spinach and dandelion, and swooned over the very smell of strawberries. Natalie cherished her mate, Frank, and let us stroke their babies, and forgave us when we gave the babies away.

When Natalie got sick we took her to the veterinarian and were told she would not get well again, so we made that choice which we human animals have granted ourselves and asked the doctor to put her to sleep. But Natalie didn't sleep. She lay in my lap and quivered and sighed and the life that she had so generously shared with us left her little round body and she was dead.

And I thought, how curious it is that this small animal could move me so, that this little life whose whole span had been but five years should make me wrestle with my conscience about the rights of humans to have charge over animals; how strange that this lifeless furry creature with the now still body should bring me to tears.

I had personified a guinea pig. I had granted her a place and dignity in my home. Somehow by my love I had elevated her to something more than a species of rodent. But she in turn had dignified me by accepting my care. She had brought beauty into our home, and had stirred in me emotions I am glad to have: love and the desire to nurture. She had trusted me and thereby had made me trustworthy.

Elizabeth Tarbox

I decided on a ferret, primarily because they are small and quiet and they don't require outdoor exercise. I found a six-month-old sable male through a newspaper ad.

I named him Root Boy—Rudy for short—because he was into everything. When I was asleep or not at home, I kept Rudy in his cage where I knew he couldn't get into trouble. However, whenever I was home, he had the run of the apartment. This meant I had to pick up after him continuously. He would pull all the books from the bottom shelf of the bookcase and root around in them, then scamper off, chirping, like he'd really enjoyed himself. He liked to play in paper bags and hide under the furniture, and all I'd see was either his tail or the end of his nose peeking out. If something was light enough for him to carry, he would hide it under the furniture, so when I did laundry I had to look everywhere for my socks and washcloths. Once I walked into the bedroom and saw my tennis shoe banging itself up against the front of my dresser. It took me a minute to realize that it was Rudy under the dresser, furiously trying to pull the shoe in after him!

I found that many people are misinformed about ferrets. They think of them as smelly rodents, wild animals who bite people. Granted, I'm sure there are some that do bite, but not all of them. Rudy was neutered and descented and raised with love and affection and never had a bad attitude.   S. R.

_____

The Bestest Housemouse Ever

…I had an unusual pet named Spot—a white mouse with black spots (hence his unusual name!)….

No one…could quite figure out how I could love a mouse so much. But Spot was so tiny and defenseless and completely trusting of me, how could I not love him? His antics and sometimes even acrobatics could keep me amused for hours. I even tried to figure out a way to make a small harness and leash so he could go outside in the summer for walks. That never did work out, though.

…Owners of unconventional pets need to know that their grief is every bit as real as owners of other types of animals….   M. G.

_____

The mice which haunted my house were not the common ones, which are said to have been introduced into the country, but a wild native kind not found in the village. I sent one to a distinguished naturalist, and it interested him much. When I was building, one of these had its nest underneath the house, and before I had laid the second floor, and swept out the shavings, would come out regularly at lunch time and pick up the crumbs at my feet. It probably had never seen a man before; and it soon became quite familiar, and would run over my shoes and up my clothes. It could readily ascend the sides of the room by short impulses, like a squirrel, which it resembled in its motions. At length, as I leaned with my elbow on the bench one day, it ran up my clothes, and along my sleeve, and round and round the paper which held my dinner, while I kept the latter close, and dodged and played at bo-peep with it; and when at last I held still a piece of cheese between my thumb and finger, it came and nibbled it, sitting in my hand, and afterward cleaned its face and paws, like a fly, and walked away.   *Henry David Thoreau [1817–62]*

For Horses

Venus and Adonis
Look, when a painter would surpass the life
In limning out a well-proportion'd steed,

His art with nature's workmanship at strife,
As if the dead the living should exceed;
   So did this horse excel a common one
   In shape, in courage, colour, pace, and bone.

Round-hooft, short-jointed, fetlocks shag and
   long,
Broad breast, full eye, small head, and nostril
   wide,
High crest, short ears, straight legs, and passing
   strong,
Thin mane, thick tail, broad buttock, tender hide:
   Look, what a horse should have he did not lack,
   Save a proud rider on so proud a back.

Sometime he scuds far off, and there he stares;
Anon he starts at stirring of a feather;
To bid the wind a base he now prepares,
And whe'r he run or fly they know not whether;
   For through his mane and tail the high wind
      sings,
   Fanning the hairs, who wave like feath'red
      wings.

William Shakespeare [1564–1616]

———————

When God created the horse he said to the magnif-
icent creature, "I have made thee unlike any other.
All the treasures of the earth lie between thy eyes.
Thou shall cast mine enemies between thy hooves,
but thou shall carry my friends on thy back. This

shall be the seat from which prayers rise up unto me. Thou shall find happiness all over the earth and thou shall be favored above all other creatures. For to thee shall accrue the love of the master of the earth, and thou shall fly without wings and conquer without a sword." *The Koran*

For Reptiles and Amphibians

The frog is a diligent songster, having a good voice but no ear. The libretto of his favorite opera, as written by Aristophanes, is brief, simple and effective—"brekekex-koäx"; the music is apparently by that eminent composer Richard Wagner.

Ambrose Bierce [1842–1914]

Two frogs I met in early childhood have lingered in my memory: I frightened one frog, and the other frog frightened me.

The frightened frog, evinced fear by placing its two hands on its head: at least, I have since understood that a frog assumes this attitude when in danger, and my frog assumed it.

The alarming frog startled me, "gave me quite a turn," as people say, by jumping when I did not know it was near me....

But seeing that matters are as they are—because frogs and suchlike cannot in reason frighten us now—is it quite certain that no day will ever come when even the smallest, weakest, most grotesque, *wronged* creature will not in some fashion rise up in the Judgement with us to condemn us, and so frighten us effectually once for all? *Christina Rossetti [1830–94]*

The Frog

Be kind and tender to the frog,
And do not call him names,
As "Slimy-Skin" or "Pollywog,"
Or likewise "Uncle James,"
Or "Gape-a-grin," or "Toad-gone-wrong,"
Or "Billy Bandy-Knees";
The frog is justly sensitive
To epithets like these.

No animal will more repay
A treatment kind and fair,
At least, so lonely people say
Who keep a frog (and by the way,
They are extremely rare). *Hilaire Belloc [1870–1953]*

The Silent Snake

The birds go fluttering in the air,
The rabbits run and skip,
Brown squirrels race along the bough,
The May flies rise and dip;
But, whilst these creatures play and leap,
The silent snake goes creepy-creep!

The birdies sing and whistle loud,
The busy insects hum,
The squirrels chat, the frogs say "croak!"
But the snake is always dumb.
With not a sound through grasses deep
The silent snake goes creepy-creep!   *author unknown*

A narrow fellow in the grass
Occasionally rides;
You may have met him,—did you not,
His notice sudden is.

The grass divides as with a comb,
A spotted shaft is seen;
And then it closes at your feet
And opens further on.

He likes a boggy acre,
A floor too cool for corn.
Yet when a child, and barefoot,
I more than once, at morn,

Have passed, I thought, a whip-lash
Unbraiding in the sun,—
When, stooping to secure it,
It wrinkled, and was gone.

Several of nature's people
I know, and they know me;
I feel for them a transport
Of cordiality;

But never met this fellow,
Attended or alone,
Without a tighter breathing,
And zero at the bone.   *Emily Dickinson [1830–86]*

A friend…offered me a most unusual challenge:
Would I be willing to adopt a young iguana who was
in need of a home?…I jumped at the chance….

The high point of our days became mealtime
when Armando would walk up my arm to retrieve
large, juicy beetles from my shoulder. He became
quite adept at finding cleverly concealed insect
morsels around the house, and before long I gave
up trying to outwit him.

When another friend appeared one day with an
elaborate, handmade leash, I thanked her but
expressed serious doubts that Armando would allow
such a device to be strapped around him…. To my
utter amazement, Armando made no fuss at all and
almost seemed to be assisting me with the curious
contraption. I was prepared to begin dragging him
toward the door when he strode bravely to the
threshold, impatiently pulling on the lead for me to
follow. The sight of a three and a half foot lizard
promenading along the sidewalk, his head held
high, with his human "owner" in tow made more
than a few neighbors stop dead in their tracks….

Although he often had to be bribed with a few
especially tasty insect treats, Armando could be

persuaded to perform for our guests. His perform-
ances often consisted of removing shoes and
sometimes even socks from unsuspecting visitors,
but once he leapt from one chair to another, land-
ing perfectly between a woman's outstretched
arms....   *B. F.*

_____

To My Pet Tortoise
My friend, you are not graceful—not at all;
Your gait's between a stagger and a sprawl.

Nor are you beautiful: your head's a snake's
To look at, and I do not doubt it aches.

As to your feet, they'd make an angel weep.
'Tis true you take them in whene'er you sleep.

No, you're not pretty, but you have, I own,
A certain firmness—mostly you're backbone.

Firmness and strength (you have a giant's thews)
Are virtues that the great know how to use—

I wish that they did not; yet, on the whole,
You lack—excuse my mentioning it—Soul.

So, to be candid, unreserved and true,
I'd rather you were I than I were you.

Perhaps, however, in a time to be,
When Man's extinct, a better world may see

Your progeny in power and control,
Due to the genesis and growth of Soul.

So I salute you as a reptile grand
Predestined to regenerate the land.

Father of Possibilities, O deign
To accept the homage of a dying reign!

In the far region of the unforeknown
I dream a tortoise upon every throne.

I see an Emperor his head withdraw
Into his carapace for fear of Law;

A King who carries something else than fat,
Howe'er acceptably he carries that;

A President not strenuously bent
On punishment of audible dissent—

Who never shot (it were a vain attack)
An armed or unarmed tortoise in the back;

Subjects and citizens that feel no need
To make the March of Mind a wild stampede;

All progress slow, contemplative, sedate,
And "Take your time" the word, in Church and
    State.

O Tortoise, 'tis a happy, happy dream,
My glorious testudinous régime!

I wish in Eden you'd brought this about
By slouching in and chasing Adam out.

Ambat Delaso

For Insects and Crawling Creatures

A Noiseless Patient Spider
A noiseless patient spider,
I mark'd where on a little promontory it stood
    isolated,
Mark'd how to explore the vacant vast
    surrounding,
It launch'd forth filament, filament, filament, out
    of itself,
Ever unreeling them, ever tirelessly speeding them.

And you O my soul where you stand,
Surrounded, detached, in measureless oceans of
    space,
Ceaselessly musing, venturing throwing, seeking
    the sphere to connect them,
Till the bridge you will need be form'd, till the
    ductile anchor hold,
Till the gossamer thread you fling catch some
    where, O my soul.   *Walt Whitman [1819–92]*

———————

Clock-a-Clay
In the cowslip pips I lie,
Hidden from the buzzing fly,

While green grass beneath me lies,
Pearled with dew like fishes' eyes,
Here I lie, a clock-a-clay,
Waiting for the time of day.

While grassy forest quakes surprise,
And the wild wind sobs and sighs,
My gold home rocks as like to fall,
On its pillar green and tall;
When the pattering rain drives by
Clock-a-clay keeps warm and dry.

Day by day and night by night,
All the week I hide from sight;
In the cowslip pips I lie,
In rain and dew still warm and dry;
Day and night, and night and day,
Red, black-spotted clock-a-clay.

My home shakes in wind and showers,
Pale green pillar topped with flowers,
Bending at the wild wind's breath,
Till I touch the grass beneath;
Here I live, lone clock-a-clay,
Watching for the time of day.

John Clare [1793–1864]

The Humble-Bee
Wiser far than human seer,
Yellow-breeched philosopher,

Seeing only what is fair,
Sipping only what is sweet,
Thou dost mock at fate and care,
    Leave the chaff and take the wheat.
When the fierce north-western blast
Cools sea and land so far and fast,
Thou already slumberest deep;
Woe and want thou cans't outsleep;
Want and woe which torture us,
Thy sleep makes ridiculous.

Ralph Waldo Emerson [1803–82]

———————

Invitation to the Bee
Child of patient industry,
Little active busy bee,
Thou art out at early morn,
Just as the opening flowers are born,
Among the green and grassy meads
Where the cowslips hang their heads;
Or by hedge-rows, while the dew
Glitters on the harebell blue.—

Then on eager wing art flown,
To thymy hillocks on the down;
Or to revel on the broom;
Or suck the clover's crimson blood;
Murmuring still thou busy bee
Thy little ode to industry!

Charlotte Smith [1749–1806]

———————

White Butterflies
Fly, white butterflies, out to sea,
Frail, pale wings for the wind to try,
Small white wings that we scarce can see,
  Fly!

Some fly light as a laugh of glee,
Some fly soft as a long, low sigh;
All to the haven where each would be,
  Fly!   *Algernon Charles Swinburne [1837–1909]*

———————

The Way to Wealth
What is a butterfly? At best
He's but a caterpillar dressed.
                Benjamin Franklin [1706–90]

———————

The Butterfly's Day
From cocoon forth a butterfly
As lady from her door
Emerged—a summer afternoon—
Repairing everywhere,

Without design, that I could trace,
Except to stray abroad
On miscellaneous enterprise
The clovers understood.

Her pretty parasol was seen
Contracting in a field
Where men made hay, then struggling hard
With an opposing cloud,

Where parties, phantom as herself,
To Nowhere seemed to go
In purposeless circumference,
As't were a tropic show.

And notwithstanding bee that worked,
And flower that zealous blew,
This audience of idleness
Disdained them, from the sky,

Till sundown crept, a steady tide,
And men that made the hay,
And afternoon, and butterfly,
Extinguished in its sea.   *Emily Dickinson [1830–86]*

To a Butterfly
Stay near me—do not take thy flight!
A little longer stay in sight!
Much converse do I find in thee,
Historian of my infancy!
Float near me; do not yet depart!
Dead times revive in thee:
Thou bring'st, gay creature as thou art!
A solemn image to my heart,
My father's family!

Oh! pleasant, pleasant were the days,
The time, when in our childish plays,
My sister Emmeline and I
Together chased the butterfly!

A very hunter did I rush
Upon the prey;—with leaps and springs
I followed on from brake to bush;
But she, God love her! Feared to brush
the dust from off its wings.

William Wordsworth [1770–1850]

The Moth
When dews fall fast, and rosy day
Fades slowly in the west away,
While evening breezes bend the future sheaves;
Votary of vesper's humid light,
The moth, pale wanderer of the night,
From his green cradle comes, amid the whispering
  leaves.
…on lacey plume
The silver moth enjoys the gloom,
Glancing on tremulous wings thro' twilight
  bowers,
Now flits where warm nasturtiums glow,
Now quivers on the jasmine bough,
And sucks with spiral tongue the balm of
  sleeping flowers.   *Charlotte Smith [1749–1806]*

Before, beside us, and above,
The firefly lights his lamp of love.

Reginald Heber [1783–1826]

A centipede was happy quite,
  Until a frog in fun

Said, "Pray, which leg comes after which?"
This raised her mind to such a pitch,
She lay distracted in the ditch
   Considering how to run.   *author unknown*

————————

The Snail
To grass or leaf, or fruit or wall,
The snail sticks close, nor fears to fall,
As if he grew there, house and all
   Together.

Within that house secure he hides,
When danger imminent betides,
Of storm, or other harm besides
   Of weather.

Give but his horns the slightest touch,
His self-collecting power is such,
He shrinks into his house with much
   Displeasure.

Where'er he dwells, he dwells alone,
Except himself, has chattels none,
Well satisfied to be his own
   Whole treasure.

Thus, hermit-like, his life he leads,
Nor partner of his banquet needs,
And if he meets one, only feeds
   The faster.

Who seeks him must be worse than blind
(He and his house are so combined),
If, finding it, he fails to find
    Its master.   *William Cowper [1731–1800]*

On the Grasshopper and the Cricket
The poetry of earth is never dead:
    When all the birds are faint with the hot sun,
    And hide in cooling trees, a voice will run
From hedge to hedge about the new-mown
        mead—
That is the Grasshopper's. He takes the lead
    In summer luxury; he has never done
    With his delights, for when tired out with fun
He rests at ease beneath some pleasant weed.

The poetry of earth is ceasing never:
    On a lone winter evening, when the frost
    Has wrought a silence, from the stove there
        shrills
The Cricket's song, in warmth increasing ever,
    And seems to one in drowsiness half lost,
    The Grasshopper's among some grassy hills.
                John Keats [1795–1821]

7

The Fragile Circle

We who choose to surround ourselves with lives even more temporary than our own, live within a fragile circle, easily and often breached. Unable to accept its awful gaps, we still would live no other way.   *Irving Townsend [1920–81]*

The simple joy that companion animals bring to our lives is priceless. When our puppy greets us at the door, she does not just wag her tail, she wags her entire body, so happy is she to be with us again—even if we had been gone only a few minutes. Birds sing their greetings; cats purr; horses whinny. Our pets cheer us, comfort us, sustain us, delight us. We treasure each of them as unique creations, learning about their "personalities," appreciating their talents, overlooking their shortcomings and failings, and loving them as they love us—unconditionally.

But we human animals understand that including pets in our lives makes of our family a fragile circle. Dogs and cats may live a dozen years, horses perhaps two dozen. We will outlive them, and their deaths will leave an aching spot in our hearts. If we continue to choose to live with pets, we will experience this grief a number of times.

When a beloved pet dies, the farewell and memorial services included in this book can give many people a sense of peace and will bring many to a sense of closure. A clergy person need not officiate, but if one is desired, the family may contact the International Association of Pet Cemeteries, the Accredited Pet Cemetery Society, or the National Association of Pet Funeral Directors for referrals to local clergy and pet cemeteries. As well, there are now websites that host virtual memorial ceremonies and tributes.

For those who feel overwhelmed with grief at the death of a pet, more and more organizations across the country are hosting pet bereavement hotlines or pet loss and bereavement counseling. Families may contact the local chapter of the American Society for the Prevention of Cruelty to Animals (ASPCA) or the Humane Society, animal shelters, any of the colleges or schools of veterinary medicine, and local veterinarians and counselors for information about pet loss support groups or hotlines. A search on the Internet for "pet loss hotline" or "pet loss support" will also turn up a number of contacts.

The pain of losing a beloved animal may raise questions about whether to adopt another pet. Will the broken heart ever dare to risk loving an animal again? The dearly departed will always hold a special place in the heart, a place no other animal will ever be able to fill. But if a family will consider it, and when a family is ready, the heart will certainly be able to grow, to admit another pet into the fragile circle, to love an animal again.

In the natural ebb and flow of life, the fragile circle expands and contracts and expands again. As we welcome another cat or dog or bird or hamster into our homes, we will begin to understand how love is the strongest force in the universe.

Through our pets, both those still with us and those who have passed on, we experience God's love firsthand. Ultimately, that is their greatest gift to us.

Appendix A

The Patron Saints of Animals

Animals	St. Francis of Assisi
Bees	Sts. Bernard and Modomnoc
Birds	Sts. Gall and Mildburga
Cattle	Sts. Baldus, Colman, and Roch
Dog Lovers	St. Roch
Domestic Animals	St. Anthony the Great
Geese	Sts. Ambrose and Martin of Tours
Horses	Sts. Colman, Eloy, George, Guy, Hippolytus, Leonard, Martin of Tours, and Stephen
Mad Dogs	St. Sithney
Sick Animals	Sts. Dwyn and Nicholas of Tolentino
Sick Cattle	Sts. Blaise, Bueno, Cornelius, and Sebastian
Sick Poultry	St. Ferreolus
Sheep	St. Wenceslaus
Swine	St. Anthony the Great
Wolves	St. Ailbe

Appendix B

Animals as Symbols for the Saints

Bees	Sts. Ambrose, Bernard, Isidore, and John Chrysostom
Beehive	St. Bernard
Birds	St. Francis of Assisi
Bull	St. Luke
Deer	St. Francis of Assisi
Dove	Sts. Ambrose, Gregory the Great, and John Chrysostom
Dragon	St. George
Eagle	St. John the Evangelist
Fish	St. Francis of Assisi
Lamb	Sts. Agnes and John the Baptist
Lion	Sts. Jerome, Mark, and Paul
Ox	St. Ambrose
Raven	St. Benedict
Swan	St. Hugh of Lincoln
Wolf	St. Francis of Assisi

Permissions and Sources

The authors have made every effort to locate the owners of copyrighted material and to secure permission to reprint. Permission to reprint copyrighted material is gratefully acknowledged as follows:

Unless otherwise indicated, all scripture quotations are from the *New Revised Standard Version Bible: Catholic Edition*, copyright © 1993 and 1989 by the Division of Christian Education of the National Council of the Churches of Christ in the U.S.A. Used by permission. All rights reserved.

Scripture quotations indicated by INT are taken from *The Inclusive New Testament*. Brentwood, MD: Priests for Equality, 1996.

Scripture quotations indicated by IP are taken from *The Inclusive Psalms*. Brentwood, MD: Priests for Equality, 1997.

Scripture quotations indicated by NJB are taken from *The New Jerusalem Bible, Reader's Edition*. New York: Doubleday, 1990. Used by permission.

Chapter 3

Prayer "We beseech you, O Lord..." adapted from the Royal Society for the Prevention of Cruelty to Animals used by permission from *Simple Blessings for Sacred Moments* by Isabel Anders, copyright © 1998, Liguori Publications, Liguori, MO 63057, www.liguori.org

Prayer "O God, I thank thee…" by George Appleton from *The Oxford Book of Prayer,* edited by George Appleton. Oxford: Oxford University Press, 1985. Used by permission.

Prayer "Heavenly Father, our human ties…" by Gloria Pinsker used by permission of the author.

Prayer "Lord God, to those…" by Edward Hays is from his *Prayers for the Domestic Church,* copyright Forest of Peace Publishing, Inc., 251 Muncie Road, Leavenworth, KS 66048. Used by permission.

Prayer "May the God who created us and you…" by (The Rev.) John Miles Evans used by permission of the author.

Chapter 4

"Saint Francis addressed [the Wolf]…" from *The Little Flowers of Saint Francis of Assisi.* Copyright © 1964, Mount Vernon, N.Y.; Peter Pauper Press. Reprinted by permission.

Prayers "O Supreme Spirit of Creation…" and "May we, in this holy pattern…" by Edward Hays are from his *Prayers for the Domestic Church,* copyright Forest of Peace Publishing, Inc., 251 Muncie Road, Leavenworth, KS 66048. Used by permission.

Prayer "Lord, make us instruments…" attributed to Saint Francis as found in *The Book of Common Prayer* (1979) of the Episcopal Church, USA.

We thank you, Lord of Heaven, for all the joys that greet us. Text: Jan Struther (1901–1953) © Oxford University Press. Used by permission. All rights reserved.

Liturgy for St. Francis Day used by permission of The Society of Saint Francis, American Province, c/o Little Portion Friary, P.O. Box 399, Mt. Sinai, NY 11766.

Selections from *CSF Office Book* used by permission of the Community of St. Francis, American Province, 3743 Cesar Chavez, San Francisco, CA 94110.

Chapter 5

"All Creatures of Our God and King" by William Draper, Copyright © 1927 J. Curwen & Sons, Ltd. All rights for the U.S. & Canada controlled by G. Schirmer, Inc. (text by St. Francis of Assisi; English translation and Music Arrangement by William Draper). International Copyright Secured. All rights reserved. Reprinted by Permission of G. Schirmer, Inc., as agents for J. Curwen & Sons, Ltd.

"Lord, Make Us Servants of Your Peace." Text: James Quinn, S.J. Text © James Quinn, S.J., Selah Publishing Co., Inc., North American agent, www.selahpub.com

"Now the Green Blade Riseth." Text: John Macleod Campbell Crum (1872–1958), © Oxford University Press. Used by permission. All rights reserved.

"Let All Things Now Living." Words copyright © 1939, 1966 by E. C. Schirmer Music Company, a division of ECS Publishing, Boston, MA. Used by permission.

Prayer "Merciful God, we turn to you in prayer…" from *Kol Haneshamah; Shirim Uvrahot: Songs and Blessings for the Home,* p. 136, The Reconstructionist Press, 7804

Montgomery Ave., Suite #9, Elkins Park, PA 19027-2649, fax: 1-215-782-8805, e-mail: press@jrf.org

Prayer "Almighty God, my soul is full…" used by permission from *The Essential Catholic Prayer Book* by Judith A. Bauer, copyright © 1999, Liguori Publications, Liguori, MO 63057, www.liguori.org

Poem "You grieve where no grief…" excerpted from *As You Grieve: Consoling Words from Around the World* by Aaron Zerah. Copyright © 2001 by Aaron Zerah. Used with permission of the publisher, Sorin Books, P.O. Box 1006, Notre Dame, IN 46556, www.sorinbooks.com

Chapter 6

Poem "Request from the Rainbow Bridge" by Constance Jenkins reprinted by permission of the author.

Meditation "It is natural to grieve…" by the Reverend Joel A. Gibson reprinted by permission of the author.

Poem "The Peace of Wild Things" from *The Selected Poems of Wendell Berry* by Wendell Berry. © 1998. Reprinted by permission of Perseus Books Group.

Poem "Stray" © 2002 by Julie Sheehan. Reprinted by permission.

Poem "A Cat" by John Gittings (Age 8) is from *Miracles: Poems by Children of the English-Speaking World.* Edited by Richard Lewis. © 1966 by Richard Lewis. Originally published by Simon and Schuster, 1966. Used with permission of Richard Lewis, The Touchstone Center, New York, NY 10128.

Poem "Heaven's Doggy-Door" © 1997 by Mary Ellen Arthur. Reprinted by permission.

Poem "She Lets Us Love Her" by James Dillet Freeman, Unity School of Christianity, 1901 NW Blue Parkway, Unity Village, MO 64605-0001. Reprinted by permission.

"The Last Will and Testament of Silverdene Emblem O'Neill" by Eugene O'Neill, from *The Unknown O'Neill*, ed. Travis Bogard, © 1988. New Haven, CT: Yale University Press. Reprinted by permission.

"I walked out alone one evening..." from The *Golden String* by Bede Griffiths. Reprinted by permission of Templegate Publishers (templegate.com), Springfield, IL.

"It happened in a park..." and "[A] friend in Hannover..." by Albert Schweitzer are from *The Ethical Mysticism of Albert Schweitzer* by Henry Clark. Copyright © 1962 by Henry Clark. Reprinted by permission of Beacon Press, Boston.

"Gentlemen of the jury..." by Senator George Graham Vest from *Dr. Johnson's Apple Orchard: The Story of America's First Pet Cemetery* by Ed Martin. © 1997 by Hartsdale Canine Cemetery, Inc., Hartsdale, NY. Used by permission.

Poem "Ringneck Parrots" by Aranda from *The Oxford Book of Animal Poems*. © 1992 by Michael Harrison and Christopher Stuart-Clark. Reprinted by permission of Oxford University Press.

"How Francis Preached to the Birds" and "[Francis] was moved by the same tender affection..." and "Once when [Francis] was staying..." from *The First Life of St. Francis* by Thomas of Celano. From *St. Francis of Assisi: Writings and Early Biographies,* ed. Marion A. Habig. © 1973 by Franciscan Press, Quincy University, Chicago. Reprinted by permission.

"I was 8 years old..." by Malcolm D. Kriger from *Dr. Johnson's Apple Orchard: The Story of America's First Pet Cemetery* by Ed Martin. © 1997 by Hartsdale Canine Cemetery, Inc., Hartsdale, NY. Used by permission.

Selections by "G.L.," "K.F.," "S.R.," "M.G.," and "B.F." from *Healing the Pain of Pet Loss: Letters in Memoriam,* ed. Kymberly Smith. © 1998. Reprinted by permission of The Charles Press, Philadelphia.

"Natalie was a gold-and-white..." by Elizabeth Tarbox from *Goodbye, Friend* by Gary Kowalski. Walpole, NH: Stillpoint Publishing, © 1997 by Gary Kowalski. Excerpted with written permission from Stillpoint Publishing.

Other Sources and References

Anders, Isabel, comp. *Simple Blessings for Sacred Moments.* Liguori, MO: Liguori/Triumph, 1998.

Arnold, Johann Christoph. *I Tell You a Mystery: Life, Death, and Eternity.* Farmington, PA: Plough Publishing Co., 1996.

Augustine, St. *Confessions.* trans. E. B. Pusey. London: Dent, 1909.

Bader, W., comp. *The Prayers of Saint Francis.* Hyde Park, NY: New City Press, 1988.

Bangs, John Kendrick. *Foothills of Parnassus.* New York: The Macmillan Co., 1914.

Barnes, Linda. casunsetz.com/dogs

Bauer, Judith, ed. and comp. *The Essential Catholic Prayer Book: A Collection of Private and Community Prayers.* Liguori, MO: Liguori, 1999.

Belloc, Hilaire. *The Bad Child's Book of Beasts.* 1896; New York: Alfred A. Knopf, 1923.

Bernardin, Joseph Buchanan, comp. *Burial Services: Rite One and Rite Two.* Wilton, CT: Morehouse-Barlow Co., 1980.

Bierce, Ambrose. *The Devil's Dictionary.* New York: Dover Publications, 1993: Ambat Delaso.

Bode, Carl, ed. *The Portable Thoreau.* New York: Penguin Books, 1985.

Book of Common Prayer and Administration of the Sacraments and Other Rites and Ceremonies of the Church, The. New York: The Seabury Press, 1977.

Brent, Hally Carrington. *Moods and Melodies.* Pittsburgh, PA: Dorrance Publishing Co., 1930.

Burroughs, John. *Birds and Poets.* New York: Hurd & Houghton/Cambridge: Riverside Press, 1877.

Campbell, Oscar James, and J. F. A. Pyre. *English Poetry of the Nineteenth Century.* New York: F. S. Crofts & Co., 1937.

Canfield, Jack, et al. *Chicken Soup for the Pet Lover's Soul: Stories about Pets as Teachers, Healers, Heroes and Friends.* Deerfield Beach, FL: Health Communications, 1998.

Clauson, J. Earl. *The Dog's Book of Verse*. Boston: Small, Maynard & Co., c. 1916.

Cleary, William. *How the Wild Things Pray*. Leavenworth, KS: Forest of Peace Publishing, 1999.

Cooke, LeBaron. *Poems*. Boston: B. Humphries, 1938.

Cotner, June. *Animal Blessings: Prayers and Poems Celebrating Our Pets*. San Francisco: Harper San Francisco, 2000: Esther Wilkin.

Curran, Stuart, ed. *The Poems of Charlotte Smith*. New York: Oxford University Press, 1993.

Daniel, Lois, ed. *The Faithful Friend: Favorite Writings about Owning and Loving Dogs*. Kansas City, MO: Hallmark, 1968.

Eddy, Sarah J., comp. *Alexander and Some Other Cats*. Boston: Marshall Jones Co., 1929.

Eliot, George. *Scenes from Clerical Life*. 1858; New York: John W. Lovell Co., 1880.

Enright, D. J., ed. *The Oxford Book of Death*. Oxford: Oxford University Press, 1983.

Exley, Helen, ed. *Cat Quotations*. New York: Exley Publications, 1992.

———. *Dog Quotations*. New York: Exley Publications, 1993.

Felleman, Hazel, comp. *The Best Loved Poems of the American People*. Garden City, NY: Garden City Books, 1936: Margaret Pollack Sherwood, Henry Dwight Sedgwick, Frank H. Selden, St. John Lucas, George Washington Doane, Josephine Preston Peabody, W. Dayton Wedgeforth, Nancy Byrd Turner.

Fitzgerald, William John. *Words of Comfort: What to Say at Times of Sadness or Loss.* Chicago: ACTA, 1999.

Francis of Assisi, St. *The Writings of St. Francis of Assisi.* Trans. Father Paschal Robinson. Philadelphia: Dolphin Press, 1906.

Franklin, Benjamin. *Poor Richard's Almanac.* Philadelphia.

Fremont, Victoria, ed. *Favorite Animal Poems.* Mineola, NY: Dover Publications, 1998: Elizabeth Turner.

Frothingham, Robert, comp. *Songs of Dogs.* Boston: Houghton Mifflin, 1920.

Frye, Mary E. "To All My Loved Ones." www.toallmyloved-ones.com.

Hardy, Thomas. *Winter Words.* New York: The Macmillan Co., 1928.

Harrison, Michael, and Christopher Stuart-Clark. *The Oxford Book of Animal Poems.* Oxford: Oxford University Press, 1992: A.S.J. Tessimond, Neil Paech, John Clare.

Hunt, Laurel E., ed. *Angel Pawprints: Reflections on Loving and Losing a Canine Companion.* Pasadena, CA: Darrowby Press, 1998.

Hymnal 1982, The. New York: The Church Hymnal Corporation, 1985.

International Network for Religion and Animals. 2913 Woodstock Ave., Silver Springs, MD 20910.

Jerome, Jerome K. (Jerome Klapka). *The Idle Thoughts of an Idle Fellow, a Book for an Idle Holiday.* New York: Scribner & Welford, 1886.

Johnston, Bertha. *Lyrical Lines for Lassie and Lad.* Brooklyn: self-published, 1923.

Joy, Charles R., trans. and ed., with introduction. *The Animal World of Albert Schweitzer: Jungle Insights into Reverence for Life.* Boston: The Beacon Press, 1950.

Kinnicutt, Lincoln, comp. *To Your Dog and to My Dog.* Boston: Houghton Mifflin, 1915.

Kol Haneshamah: Daily. Wyncote, PA: The Reconstructionist Press, 1996.

Kol Haneshamah: Shabbat Vehagim. Wyncote, PA: The Reconstructionist Press, 1996. Shmuel Hanagid.

Kol Haneshamah: Songs, Blessings and Rituals for the Home. Wyncote, PA: The Reconstructionist Press, 1991.

Kowalski, Gary. *Goodbye, Friend: Healing Wisdom for Anyone Who Has Ever Lost a Pet.* Walpole, NH: Stillpoint Publishing, 1997.

Lawrence, D. H. *Birds, Beasts and Flowers!* London: M. Secker, 1923.

Lemieux, Christina M. *Coping with the Loss of a Pet: A Gentle Guide for All Who Love a Pet.* Reading, PA: Wallace R. Clark & Co., 1992.

Little Flowers of Saint Francis of Assisi, The. Translated by Abby Langdon Alger. Mount Vernon, NY: The Peter Pauper Press, 1964.

Martin, Edward C., Jr. *Dr. Johnson's Apple Orchard: The Story of America's First Pet Cemetery.* Hartsdale, NY: Hartsdale Canine Cemetery, Inc., 1997.

Martin, Robert Bernard, ed. *Victorian Poetry: Ten Major Poets.* New York: Random House, 1964.

Méry, Fernand. *The Life, History, and Magic of the Cat.* New York: Madison Square Press, 1968.

Miller, Robert J., with Stephen J. Hrycyniak. *GriefQuest: Men Coping with Loss*. Winona, MN: Saint Mary's Press, 1996.

Montgomery, Mary, and Herb Montgomery. *Good-bye, My Friend: Grieving the Loss of a Pet*. Minneapolis, MN: Montgomery Press, 1999.

Nieburg, Herbert A., and Arlene Fischer. *Pet Loss: A Thoughtful Guide for Adults and Children*. New York: HarperPerennial, 1982.

O'Cotter, Pat [Frank J. Cotter]. *Rhymes of a Roughneck*. Seward, AK: self-published, 1918.

Plato. *The Republic*. Translated by Allan Bloom. New York: Basic Books, 1968.

Raleigh, Sir Walter. "As You Came from the Holy Land."

Reath, Mary, comp. *Public Lives, Private Prayers*. Notre Dame, IN: Sorin Books, 2001.

Richardson, Robert. "In Willow and Wattle," 1893.

Rossetti, Christina. *Time Flies: A Reading Diary*. London: SPCK, 1885.

Schweitzer, Albert. *Aus meiner Kindheit und Jugendzeit*. Munich: C. H. Beck'sche Verlagsbuchhandlung, 1926. (Published in English as *Memoirs of Childhood and Youth*. New York: The Macmillan Co., 1931.)

———. "The Ethics of Reverence for Life." *Christendom* I:2 (Winter 1936).

———. *Zwischen Wasser und Urwald*. Bern: Paul Haupt, 1926. (Published in English as *On the Edge of the Primeval Forest*. New York: The Macmillan Co., 1931.)

Shakespeare, William. *The Complete Works*. New York: Barnes & Noble Books, 1994: Sonnet 73; "Venus and Adonis."

Sherwood, Margaret Pollock. *The Upper Slopes*. Boston: Houghton Mifflin, 1924.

Sife, Wallace. *The Loss of a Pet: A Guide to Coping with the Grieving Process When a Pet Dies*. New York: Howell Book House, 1998.

Smith, Kymberly, ed. *Healing the Pain of Pet Loss: Letters in Memoriam*. Philadelphia: The Charles Press, 1998.

Society of St. Francis, American Province, Little Portion Friary, P.O. Box 399, Mt. Sinai, NY 11766, www.societystfrancis.org.

Spofford, Ainsworth R., and Charles Gibbon. *The Library of Choice Literature and Encyclopaedia of Universal Authorship*. 2 vols. Philadelphia: The Gebbie Publishing Co., 1895.

Stanfield, Leontine. *Leontine Stanfield's Book of Verse*. New York: J. S. Ogilvie Publishing Co., 1906.

Thomas of Celano, The First Life of St. Francis. In *St. Francis of Assisi: Writings and Early Biographies*. Marion A. Habig, ed. Chicago: Franciscan Press, 1973.

Ulanov, Barry, comp. *On Death: Wisdom and Consolation from the World's Great Writers*. Liguori, MO: Triumph Books, 1996.

Virgil. *Aeneid*, trans. John Dryden.

Zerah, Aaron. *As You Grieve: Consoling Words from Around the World*. Notre Dame, IN: Sorin Books, 2001.